The Art of Silk Ribbon Embroidery

By Judith Baker Montano

C&T PUBLISHING

©1993 by Judith Baker Montano

All photographs in the Silk Ribbon Stitch Guide by Judith Baker
    Montano, Castle Rock, Colorado, unless otherwise credited

Illustrations by Judith Baker Montano

Cover concept by Judith Baker Montano
    Cover photographed by Bill O'Connor, Denver, Colorado
    Cover production by Rose Sheifer Graphic Productions,
        Walnut Creek, California

Edited by Louise O. Townsend

Technical editing by Elizabeth Aneloski

Design and production coordination by Diana L. Grinwis,
    Grinwis Art Service, East Lansing, Michigan

Published by C & T Publishing,
    P. O. Box 1456, Lafayette, California 94549

ISBN 0-914881-55-8

Library of Congress Cataloging-in-Publication Data

Montano, Judith Baker
    The art of silk ribbon embroidery / by Judith Baker Montano.
        p.   cm.
    Includes bibliographical references.
    ISBN 0-914881-55-8 : $19.95
    1. Silk ribbon embroidery.   I. Title.
TT778.S64M65   1993
746.44—dc20   92-53801
                        CIP

Ceramcoat™ is a trademark of Delta/Shiva
Igolochkoy™ is a trademark of Birdhouse Enterprises
Natesh® is a registered trademark of Kaleidoscope
Nymo® is a registered trademark of Belding Heminway Co., Inc.
Pellon® is a registered trademark of Freudenberg Nonwovens,
    Pellon Division
Tacky Glue® is a registered trademark of Artis, Inc.
Velcro® is a registered trademark of Velcro USA, Inc.

Printed in Hong Kong

10   9   8

Dedication

For
my two
mothers,
Muriel & Joyce

Thanks
to you,
"This Cowgirl
is a Lady"

Table of Contents

Projects

Silk Ribbon Stitch Guide

Source Guide

Foreword

 rom the very first time I saw Judith's work I was captivated by her intertwining of stitches, beads, and ribbons in the embroidery that is so much her style. She has a way of combining techniques and materials that makes the ornamentation rich in color and texture.

Judith brings a vast background of knowledge and life experience to her work. The foundation is the cloth, and she builds on this with the texture of beads, ribbons, and stitching until a dimensional quality emerges. It exemplifies creativity at its finest while being a true expression of self.

The Art of Silk Ribbon Embroidery revives and documents the ancient embroidery techniques begun in the 1700s in France. Judith's personal presentation encourages the reader to feel she is having a private stitching session. Careful attention is paid to the detailing of project instructions as well as the use of materials. Through her travels to Japan, England, and Australia, Judith has discovered how others stitch. This experience is brought out in the text. She has created a centerpiece worth preserving for time in the revival of silk ribbon embroidery techniques.

— *Jean Wells*

 either stodgy rules nor tedious theories here — just an exuberant look at a charming, antique embroidery form, which Judith Montano transforms into subtle or dynamic texture for contemporary stitchery. Flatly stating that she goes more for effect than technique, Judith leads us through a wealth of lore, process, illustration, sources, tips, and projects to revitalize a very old delicacy: ribbon embroidery.

It is fortuitous that Judith brings this fascinating embroidery around again just as diminutive silk ribbons are amply available from Japan and France in a stunning array of colors, and when fibers artists are seeking new adventures in expression. We may sigh over 18th-century gowns and petticoats and marvel at Victorian court trains. But we are dazzled by the 20th-century quilts made by Montano and friends, on which silk ribbons explode with color as they dance across fabric with unique lustre and pattern. The author's enormous enthusiasm and love of her subject make anything seem possible. It's a tempting come-on, and I predict acres of silken roses and other ribbon enchantments as you pursue this embroidery revival. This beautiful book gives you all the help and inspiration you'll ever need.

— *Wilcke Smith*

Acknowledgments

eedlework has always been a mixed blessing for me. It was the bane of my existence as a young girl and the opening to the doors of the world as an adult. If I had been told as a young girl that my needlework skills would cause me to write books, lecture all over the world, and design original art garments, I would have just shrugged my shoulders and rode off on my horse! And my mother would have fainted in disbelief!

I was an impossible student, far more interested in playing outside with my horse and working the cattle with my dad, but Mom persisted and managed to teach me the basic lazy daisy and stem stitches. During the winter months I embroidered tea towels and pillowcases for my hope chest — I was hopeless, but Mom was relentless, and eventually I mastered fancy stitches like the feather stitch and cretan. It was a triumph in perseverance and patience for us both. Over the years she managed to teach my sisters and me the basics of knitting, cross stitch, needlepoint, and crochet.

All of my embroidery and needlework skills, except for one, were moved to the back burner when I went off to university. My goal was to be an artist, using pen and ink and oils as my media. The only needlework skill that stood me in good stead was crochet. Afghans were very popular in my university years, and in our sorority, if we didn't have a date, we'd stay in and work on our afghans. Thanks to my mother, I had the basics of crochet down pat and thanks to my less than sparkling social life, I produced several afghans!

As the years progressed my art career took a sidetrack into the quilting world. I discovered crazy quilting, and embroidery took on a new importance. Through this varied and colorful technique, I have met wonderful people from all over the world. We remain friends because of a shared love — needlework — and because of these friends I keep learning new needlework techniques.

I want to thank the following people for their support and encouragement. I could not continue without them.

❋ Muriel Bigland Hays — my beloved aunt and godmother has always been there for me — she gives me endless love and encouragement.

❋ Joyce Van Winkle Baker — my dear mother. Her love and talent for needlework has always been an inspiration to me.

❋ My Family — I love you all. You are my one mainstay in life.

❋ Kaethe Kliot — for her gracious advice and help in creating this book. She is a true expert in the needlework field.

❋ Carolie and Tom Hensley, Todd and Tony Hensley — my special family of friends at C & T Publishing.

❋ Editor Louise Townsend, photographer Bill O'Connor, and designer Diana Grinwis, my professional friends who make the job of author a little easier.

❋ A special "Thank You" to the following for their friendship, assistance, and inspiration: Jean Fox, Heather Joynes, Merrilyn Heazelwood, Jenny Bradford, Ruth Stonely, Imelda DeGraw, Donna V. Porter, Denise Brice, Wilanna Bristow, Jan McCormick, Marie Platt, Pam Smith, Yvonne Porcella, Lynn Bowden, Remona Gibeson, Gloria McKinnon, Etsuko Kamatsu, Kaye Pyke, Frances Vesper, Jane Mueller, Ruth Madrid, Shannon Gimble, Jason Montano, Madeleine Montano, Sarah Smith, Michaelá Kovacs, Alexandra Lober, and Katheryn Sipple.

Introduction

I discovered silk ribbon embroidery several years ago while teaching at the Houston Quilt Festival, when Jean Fox of San Benito, Texas, showed me a piece she was working on. I was fascinated with the dimensional effect of the ribbon.

Months later, I taught for Jean's quilt guild and stayed in her home. She is an avid crazy quilter and collector of antique sewing tools and accessories. Among her collection is a large selection of Chinese sewing baskets. Upon opening a small basket, I discovered a needle case decorated with silk ribbon roses. I was completely taken with the delicate flowers and asked her to teach me the technique. Jean showed me several pages from an early ladies magazine that showed ribbon embroidery stitches, and she demonstrated a few basic stitches for me. We made copies of the instructions, and I had good intentions of practicing, but the silk ribbon was impossible to find, I was busy as a teacher, and so the pages were filed away.

A few months later, I made my first Australian tour. Everywhere I went, the Australian women were doing silk ribbon embroidery — beautiful, delicate work on linen, blankets, and clothing. Because all types of embroideries were the norm, they were able to buy 4mm silk ribbon more easily than in the United States and Canada. When my friend Gloria McKinnon of Anne's Glory Box in Newcastle, Australia, presented me with a silk ribbon embroidery book by Heather Joynes, I was chafing at the bit to get started.

Two months later, I was off to Japan for a teaching tour. One of my students was Professor Suzuki — she called the people at a local silk company to come and view my work. When they heard that I used silk buttonhole twist for my embroidery work, they presented me with a gift box of silk threads and ribbon. I started experimenting with the ribbons that day and soon discovered that I could use it in the same way as the silk threads. Imagine my delight, when a few weeks later, I was contracted to be the official endorser of their silk threads and ribbon! It was the beginning of a wonderful friendship.

On my second Australian tour, I met Jenny Bradford in my Canberra class. She is a silk ribbon embroidery expert, and has written many marvelous books on the craft. We admired each other's work, and I went home from that class with the idea that crazy quilting and silk ribbon embroidery could be combined.

Through my favorite method of learning — trial and error — I practiced during the coming year with my pathetic attempts at silk ribbon embroidery. Thanks to the Japanese silk company, Heather Joynes, and Jenny Bradford, I had an array of ribbons and clear concise instructions.

To say that silk ribbon embroidery is addictive is an understatement. It takes over all other interests. Not only is it fast and effective, but it is delicate and pretty. I was embroidering silk flowers all over my crazy quilt pieces and soon discovered that it could be combined with punch needle embroidery and beading. I was truly hooked.

On my third Australian tour, I was anxious for a professional lesson as I felt my attempts were amateurish. Kay Ross of Brisbane, an expert ribbon embroideress, met with me after a class, and we had a midnight lesson. She was wonderful and very encouraging. It gave me the confidence to continue, and she showed me some special techniques like the pistil stitch, the loop stitch and the lazy daisy with bullion tip. I practiced all the way back to Los Angeles — a 14-hour trip!

Because I am self-taught and have a dyslexic problem of left and right, I have come up with my own style. I tend to go more for the effect than the technique. Through the encouragement of Kaethe Kliot of Lacis, a marvelous needlework shop in Berkeley, California, I've decided to write this book. So, I'm presenting silk ribbon work to you, not as an expert in this technique, but as someone who truly loves it. I want you to enjoy it as much as I do. My goal is to introduce you to experts in the field and to the history of this beautiful craft. I've included a large, concise stitch dictionary, 12 patterns, and lots of color photographs to inspire you.

So, please join me in exploring the world of silk ribbon embroidery. And please do not hold me responsible if you become hooked on this craft. I have given you fair warning!

Background & History

French Beginnings

The history of silk ribbon embroidery is a difficult path to follow as so little is recorded in needlework and history books. I've spent countless hours hunched over volumes of *Godey's* ladies magazines (1840 to 1893) gleaning one or two paragraphs and viewing lots of color plates of floral decoration but no embroidery. Searching through the Denver Art Museum Needlework Library, I found silk ribbon embroidery mentioned here and there with little importance given to it.

Thanks to Kaethe Kliot of Lacis in Berkeley, California, and her extensive library, I was able to follow the erratic path of silk ribbon embroidery. I've come to the conclusion that it is a needle art that reappears periodically and is passed by word of mouth (mother to daughter, friend to friend) more than by any other means.

Silk ribbon embroidery (ribbon work, Rococo embroidery) first appeared in France during the Rococo era of the 1700s. From 1750 to 1780, fashions called for elaborate dress decoration of ribbons, flowers, and ruching applied by embroidery. Royalty and court ladies wore gowns festooned with silk ribbon embroidery. The court dresses of the day featured large panniers. These were perfect to show off the elaborate floral sprays of silk and chiffon ribbon.

Only royalty and the court could afford to wear such elaborate garments. These were produced by "official" embroidery houses and took months of labor. Under the patronage of the French kings, the couture houses thrived. Soon the fashion of the French court drifted to England, and silk ribbon embroidery became a fashionable statement for the ladies of the British court. From there it moved to British colonies such as the United States, Canada, Australia, and New Zealand.

American Nightcap made of silk ribbon embroidery and silk flat ribbons and lace, circa 1870s. (*From the collection of Takeo Maejima. Photo: Judith Montano*)

Shaded Ribbon Work by Frances Vesper, taught to do silk ribbon work by her aunt, who in turn was trained in the late 1800s in France. Mrs. Vesper works with antique variegated French silk ribbon to make these delicate pieces. (*Photo: Sharon Risedorph*)

The Moravians

From Georgina Brown Harbeson, author of *American Needlework — The History of Decorative Stitchery and Embroidery from the late-16th to the 20th Century*, we learn in the 1700s of a Czechoslovakian group known as Moravians who settled in Georgia and Pennsylvania. They were a religious, pacifist group, and the women were renowned for their beautiful needlework. This group founded the Sisters of Bethlehem and set up a school for needlework in 1750. They taught all types of needlework, floral embroidery, crépe work, and ribbon work.

A Moravian bridal dress from the 1790s is described as follows: "The white satin is ornamented with ribbon work and small pieces of gauze formed into roses. It belongs to the period of high waists and short puffed sleeves. In the customary fashion, the bride wore over this gown a white embroidered gauze shawl of triangular shape, one corner of which is elaborately embroidered."

American Silk Trade

Silk was produced in America in the early 1800s. Many women spun their own silk from their cottage grown cocoons. Silk sewing thread was made in the state of Massachusetts in the early 1800s.

The silk worm depends on the mulberry leaf for food, and mulberry trees were grown in numerous states, thanks to the foresight of Doctor Stiles, the president of Yale College. He sent seeds all over the United States in hope of building a large silk industry. The Moravians were very busy with silk cultivation in Bethlehem, Pennsylvania, and the Quakers in Lancaster County also cultivated silk. In 1770, an American woman named Susannah Wright gained recognition when her silk was made into a court dress for the Queen of England. In the 1830s, braids, ribbons and silk trims were being produced by the Mansfield Company in Connecticut.

1838 saw the beginning of the Mt. Nebo silk mills in South Manchester, Connecticut. They produced the first factory silk and grew their own mulberry trees along with huge cocooneries. By 1840 the silk mania was rampant from new England to Florida. Unfortunately, hopes and dreams were shattered when the mulberry tree proved difficult to cultivate and the introduction of cheaper silk from the Orient brought American sales to a standstill.

Floral Spray: Violets and Nicotine Flowers

1870 Revival

Ribbon embroidery in 1870 saw a new revival. This was probably due to the French silk ribbons introduced by designer Michonet. They came in beautiful, variegated shades. The technique is referred to in the *Ladies Guide to Needlework* (1877) by Annie Frost:

"Embroidery in Narrow Ribbon — the ribbons to be used are the various shaded ones to be bought at most dry goods shops. The design is traced upon the material to be worked, and as each stitch forms a petal leaf, the design must not be too elaborate; small rosettes are prettier than large ones. The ribbon is to be threaded through a large wool needle, and worked as you would silk or wool. For the stems, tendrils, centers of flowers, etc., colored silk must be used."

Silk ribbon work appeared in crazy quilts, domestic decorations, millinery, and clothing. Reference to little round hats decorated with ostrich feathers and ribbons is made in *American Needlework*. The ribbons were wide enough to carry sprays of flowers upon them, embroidered with smaller ribbons and arasene (a kind of mixed thread of wool and silk used in raised embroidery).

A reference in *Peterson's* magazine in December 1882 was made to arasene ribbons in the decoration of parasols and ball gowns: "When real lace is inserted to soften a high-collared neckline, the ribbon embroidery extends its dainty leaves and flowers upon it, thus tying foundation materials and trimmings into a shimmering unity of design."

In a small 15¢ pamphlet, "Ornamented Stitches for Embroidery," published in the early 1900s for *Comfort* magazine of Augusta, Maine, ribbon embroidery is mentioned as a way of further decorating crazy quilting.

"The best flowers for this work are those in which each petal can be covered by a single piece of ribbon, as the wild rose, forget-me-not, wild clematis, daisy, Russian snow flower, etc. The method of working is as follows:

'For a rose, take five shades of rose pink grosgrain ribbon No. 9, cut fine pieces (one of each shade) two inches long; commence it with the darkest shade; make two small plaits in one end and tack it on the outer end of the petal; then bring the other end of the ribbon over and pass it down through a slit made in the center of the rose, being careful to draw the selvages a little tighter than the center, in order to make the petal stand out, soft and puffy; make the other petals in the same manner, then fill the center with French knots of maize embroidery silk, also make the stamens by carrying stitches of silk up onto the ribbon with a French knot at the end, to represent the pollen. For finer flowers like forget-me-nots, the ribbon may be threaded into a large-sized worsted needle, and worked through and through, taking a small stitch for each petal.' "

From *Peterson's* (1880), an article by Mrs. Jane Weaver sings the praises for shaded ribbon embroidery. She mentions a silk ribbon embroidery pattern offered in *Peterson's* January 1877 issue, but tells the reader that the use of shaded ribbon has raised this kind of embroidery to the level of art needlework: "Hardly any floral device is too intricate in outline and color to be executed in ribbon embroidery. But the special province for this kind of work seems to us to be the reproduction of floral scrolls and graceful bouquets of late Renaissance and early Rococo period, which are just now so much in vogue for dress trimmings and decorative needlework generally. Ribbon work is very effective for court trains, shoulder sashes, polonaise trimmings, and shows well on both light and dark materials, provided the colors of ground and of embroidery are artistically contrasted."

Antique-Style Flowers by Jean Fox. A spray of satin and silk flowers add a delicate beauty to her velvet vest.
(Photo: Britton's Photo)

Australian Work

In Australia, the popularity of Victorian ribbon work spread from clothing to cushions, screens, hankies and glove sachets. Jennifer Isaacs, author of *The Gentle Arts, 200 Years of Australian Women's Domestic and Decorative Arts* (1987) tells us that Australian women favored ribbon work on cushion covers and mantle drapes. They worked with ⅛" shaded — pale to dark — silk ribbon which was relatively cheap and available in preprinted kits from England and America. The designs were printed on linen or fabric of choice, ready to work with needles and packs of ribbon. They were also available with iron-on transfers.

Weldons, a Victorian needlework magazine, offered instructions for making sprays of gathered flowers and baskets of flowers. The silk ribbon was gathered along one side and pulled up in a puckered mass. The ribbon was sewn down in a spiral shape. A malore of steel or ivory was used for holding down the ribbons, to prevent twisting. Most of the Australian patterns were of English flowers and designs.

Antique-Style Flowers by Jean Fox. Gathered, ruched, and embroidered silk and satin flowers form a bouquet of old-fashioned beauty. *(Photo: Judith Montano)*

China Ribbon

eferences to China ribbon often appeared, and as early as 1842 it was used for flowers and leaves. Silk thread was run along one edge, pulled up into the desired shape and applied upon satin foundations for pictures and costumes. In the late 1800s, *Caufield's Dictionary of Needlework* defines China ribbon as a "very narrow ribbon, of about ⅛", woven with a plain edge and to be had in one color, or shaded gradually from a dark to a light tint of any color. This work was largely employed for decorative purposes during the earlier part of the present century and has lately reappeared under the title of Rococo and Ribbon Embroidery." It goes on to point out the importance of keeping the flowers in proportion and to keep the ribbon flat. Also presented is a 50-year-old pattern for a sachet or handbag made of forget-me-not floral sprays, roses, and daisies.

The 1880s and 1890s saw the most extensive use of ribbon work on ball gowns and elaborate evening costumes. Usually antique pastels in color, the embroidery resembled the costume embroideries of the 18th century in France. Pale rose, dusty rose, sage green, faded purple, and pale-pink violet were the most popular colors. Ribbon work was applied to cuffs and collars of children's dresses

1930s Dressing Gown. Madaleine Montano wears a 60-year-old dressing gown decorated with satin ribbon folded flowers and embroidery. *(Photo: Judith Montano)*

as well as to adult costumes. Favorite flowers were heartsease, fuchsias, convolvulus, and moss roses. Slowly the art of ribbon embroidery died out. *The Art Needlework Book* of 1900 put it this way: "There is less objection to embroidery in ribbon, which also had its day in the 18th century. It was very much the fashion for court dresses under Louis Seize 'Broderie de faveur' as it was called, whence our 'lady's faveur' — faveur being a narrow ribbon. Some beautiful work of its kind was done in ribbon, sometimes shaded.

"The effect of ribbon work is happiest when it is not sewn through the stuff after the manner of satin stitch, but lies on the surface of the satin ground and is only just caught down at the ends of the loops, which go to make leaves and petals. The twist of the ribbon where it turns gives interest to the

Ladies in Dresses. Fashion magazines were popular during the Victorian era. Here are three beautiful dresses, including a ball gown with ribbon roses. *(Photo: Courtesy of Judith Montano)*

surface of the embroidery. An effect of ribbon work, but of a harder kind, was produced by onlaying strips of cord upon a silken ground, twisted about after the fashion of ribbon. Neither it nor ribbon embroidery is of any serious account."

1907 Revival

 uckily, *The Art in Needlework* was completely wrong, for ribbon embroidery made another grand revival in 1907. This time the designs were much bolder with less embroidery and more trim made by couching and appliqué of ribbon work.

In the 1920s, the French town of Bovier was famous for its evening bags, gloves, and accessories, highly decorated in silk ribbon embroidery. During this same period the fashion house of Boué Soeurs in Paris was producing gowns festooned with beautiful ribbon work.

Present History

 ntil the late 1980s the art of silk ribbon embroidery has remained dormant, quietly being worked in various parts of America, Australia, and New Zealand. It has remained popular with some doll makers

and makers of heirloom garments. The current revival is due entirely to the ribbon workers in Australia where the gentle art of needlework is still a very important part of their culture.

Two pioneers of ribbon embroidery in Australia are Heather Joynes and Jenny Bradford. Both have been forerunners in this field, teaching and producing books on the subject. Please notice their work in the following profiles section. Adding to the popularity of ribbon work is the vast array of silk ribbons now available from Japan.

The interest in Victoriana and days gone by also attests to the renewed popularity of silk ribbon embroidery. Women are interested in Victorian needlework and decoration making the art of silk ribbon embroidery a perfect choice.

Ribbon and Metallic Thread Appliqué. Purchased appliqués were popular during the Victorian era. Here are two examples featuring ribbon flowers. Notice the cigarette silks in the background. *(Photo: Judith Montano)*

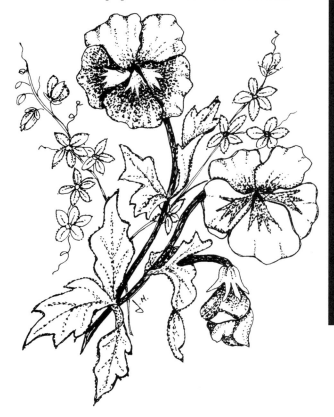

Profiles

It is with great pride and pleasure that I introduce to you twelve interesting women who weave silk ribbon embroidery into inspiring pieces of needlework. Some of them are authors and professional teachers. Some teach locally and internationally; some of them practice ribbon art as a hobby. They come from all walks of life. All of them share a love of needlework, and they are eager to share their ideas and skills. A few of the women hold full-time jobs, and silk ribbon embroidery is juggled in with families and other duties. All of them find it a very rewarding and inspiring creative form and when asked why they do it, everyone echoed, "because I love it!"

I have listed addresses for these women in the back of the book under "Teachers" in the source chapter. Please contact them for catalogs, teaching information, and inspiration. I know you will enjoy "meeting" each and every one of them.

— Judith

Lynne Bowden

ynne Bowden is an accomplished needle-woman who has been keenly interested in an assortment of techniques for 20 years. She was born in Nelson on the South Island of New Zealand, moving to Hamilton on the North Island at the age of 13.

Lynne adores flowers and reproduces them through needlework. She designs gardens, collects old-fashioned roses, and decorates her home with antiques. At the age of 6, she made a burlap (hessian) potholder, embroidered with wool, but credits her sister with introducing her 20 years ago to counted cross stitch and the design work of Clara Weaver of Denmark.

Lynne claims she does not have a family background in embroidery, but her father did embroider two cushions while convalescing from an illness before and during World War II. Lynne enjoys the constant encouragement of her husband and daughters. He is very often involved with the design and technical difficulties of some of her projects. Above all the family encourages her attendance at embroidery classes.

Lynne is a busy woman, balancing family and a career of organizing and practicing specialty-surgery nursing. She started silk ribbon embroidery three years ago and claims she is a traditionalist, using it on cushions, clothing, accessories, and heirloom sewing. She teaches only four classes a year and these are weekend, project-oriented classes. She always encourages her students to design for themselves. She has received great acclaim for a nine-piece ensemble of which the jacket is the main feature. All of these pieces were made from three new silk curtains given to Lynne by an interior decorator friend.

Lynne credits silk ribbon embroidery with making her invest $1,500 in ribbon during two years, disrupting the house-hold, bringing her unbelievable attention, and turning her into a stitch-a-holic who must embellish everything in sight!

Jenny Bradford

orn and educated in England with a teach-ing diploma from Cambridge University, Jenny Bradford and her family immigrated to Australia in 1964. She has been involved in needlework since she was a child and has become a known expert in many facets of needlecraft, teaching throughout England, the United States, and Australia. Taught by her grandmother to do Fair Isle knit-ting before the age of 10, Jenny cannot remember a time when she was not involved in creating articles in fabric and thread.

After moving to Canberra in 1983, Jenny specialized in smocking and branched out into writing books on the subject (*Simply Smocking* and *Simply Smocking 2*). In recent years, Jenny has been instrumental in the re-introduction and promotion of silk ribbon embroi-dery and her four books on the subject (*Silk Ribbon Embroidery — Australian Wildflower Designs*; *Silk Ribbon Embroidery 2 — Transform your Clothes*; *Silk Ribbon Embroidery for Gifts and Garments*; and *Original Designs For Silk Ribbon Embroidery*) published and printed in Australia, have boosted the popularity of this lovely craft.

Jenny is well-known for her creative workshops, which vary from one to four days (six hours each). The first day is always devoted to learning techniques and working samples.

Jenny's introduction to silk ribbon embroidery was quite accidental. She was teaching a smocking class in 1986 when one of her students asked if she had ever heard of silk ribbon embroidery. The student was orga-nizing a workshop the following week to be given by Melva McCameron. The following weekend Jenny attended the class, and she's been hooked on silk ribbon embroidery ever since.

Jenny says she owes a great deal to silk ribbon embroi-dery because it has completely changed her life, giving her the opportunity to produce a series of books that are widely used internationally as teaching manuals for silk ribbon embroidery, to travel, and to meet many interest-ing people. Students and friends are very pleased that Jenny has brought silk ribbon embroidery to the forefront and that she is continuing to write books on the subject.

PHOTO: YVONNE QUMI

Denise Brice

Denise Brice is as feminine and delicate as her beautiful needlework. Born in Northcote, Victoria, Australia, into a family of three daughters, she learned basic needlework at a young age. Her mother was a proficient dressmaker. She gained a love of sewing by watching her mother and grandmother spend many hours creating beautiful things. Her first embroidery teacher was her Aunty Lorraine who spent many hours one night in Adelaide on the wrong side of midnight teaching her to do bullion roses!

Denise saw her first piece of silk ribbon embroidery in an antique shop and couldn't get it out of her mind. She went back to the shop to buy it, but it was gone. She went to the local museum to see what she could find out about silk ribbon embroidery, and this was the beginning of a passion.

She says "My first real piece of embroidery was a baby's singlet embroidered at the neckline with bullion roses and French knots. The roses looked more like tired old carnations but I was 'hooked.' I wish I had kept that first piece to show my students."

Denise is not a traditionalist in the true sense as her work is more free-flowing. She uses silk ribbon in many ways from embellishing garments to creating three-dimensional effects using painted backgrounds for embroidered gardens and landscapes.

Denise teaches three classes a week and is very involved in workshops and symposiums. She has been featured in Australia's *Craft and Home* magazine and the Don Caster and Templestowe News. Her classes are in three-hour intervals and last four weeks. She also conducts half- and full-day workshops. She offers project- and design-oriented classes and travels internationally. Denise's family supports her fully in her needle art pursuits, and above all they understand her passion for embroidery.

Denise's needlework shows a love of nostalgia and the charm of bygone days. She feels that silk ribbon embroidery captures that charm and reflects inner peace not often found in today's busy lifestyle.

Wilanna Bristow

Wilanna Bristow is a well-known American needlework expert from San Antonio, Texas. She was raised on a farm near Lockhart, Texas, where her mother was a teacher and her father a farmer. This allowed Wilanna a lot of creative time. By the age of 6, she was using an old Singer sewing machine to make doll clothes out of lace — laces removed from her grandmother's elegant garments. Wilanna has carried on with a needle in her hand ever since those early days.

This talented lady began the serious study of embroidery during her newborn daughter's naps in 1963. During the early years, she was primarily self-taught — but her love of needlework soon connected her to Erica Wilson and private lessons in Florence, Italy, and the Lysée D' Enseignement Professionel in Paris, France, a school specializing in couture embroidery. Wilanna has co-authored *Patterns With Potential, Fundamentals of Color* (a color-correspondence course for the Embroiderers Guild of America), and she has written the final chapter of *The Sublime Heritage of Martha Mood*.

She has numerous pieces appearing in publications by Erica Wilson, Sarita Rainey, and Jean Ray Laury.

Wilanna fell in love with silk ribbon embroidery upon viewing the Boué Soeurs court presentation dress at the Costume Institute in New York and tried to reproduce the ribbon flowers for her daughter's wed-

PHOTO: ANSEN SEALE

ding dress in 1988. She is a long-standing member of the Embroiderers Guild of America. Her work is included in the Library of the Costume Institute of the Metropolitan Museum of Art in New York City, in the Archives of American Art in Washington, D.C., and in the LBJ Library in Austin, Texas. She teaches silk ribbon embroidery professionally as one of many techniques for couture embellishment. Her classes are tailored to a group's needs on stitching level and vary from one to four days. She teaches nationally and internationally.

Right: Blue-gray silk curtain fabric is the background for this elegant jacket. Lynne Bowden of Hamilton, New Zealand, has decorated the jacket with garlands of soft, delicate roses, daisies, fuchsias, forget-me-nots, baby's breath, and ribbon bows. Lynn is noted for her profusion of silk ribbon embroidered bouquets. *(Photo: Bill Lindberg Photography)*

Above: Jenny Bradford is a prolific author and embroideress from Canberra, Australia. Columbines and butterflies circle a wooden clock keeping time with grace and beauty. *(Photo: Andre Martin)*

Right: Denise Brice is known for her painted cottages and teddy bears. She comes from Melbourne, Australia, and has been combining embroidery, silk work, and painting for years. *(Photo: Yvonne Qumi)*

Above: Wilanna Bristow of San Antonio, Texas, produces wondrous works in silk ribbon. Here is an elegant plum vest with flowers made from antique silk ribbons. Ombre ribbon weaves throughout the three-dimensional flowers. *(Photo: Ansen Seale)*

Above right: In this wall hanging that will please both quilters and embroiderers, Gloria McKinnon of Newcastle, N.S.W., Australia, has used silk ribbon embroidery to embellish patterns from *Australian Houses in Patchwork* by Margaret Rolfe and Beryl Hodges. Here, four pieced houses are decorated with silk ribbon flowers. *(Photo: Alan Carter)*

Right: Kaye Pyke of Melbourne, Australia, has added elegance and vitality to the art of silk ribbon embroidery. Her cushions and pillows are eagerly sought after. Here is a beautiful example of Kaye's work — a damask monogrammed pillow highlighted with a crest of roses. *(Photo: Neil Lorimer)*

Left: Here is a lovely sampler of roses by Merrilyn Heazelwood of Tasmania, Australia. Merrilyn is well-known for her silk ribbon embroidery books featuring flowers. *(Photo: Courtesy of Merrilyn Heazelwood)*

Right: Here is a beautiful collection of antique-style ribbon embroidery by Frances Vesper of Carmichael, California. Mrs. Vesper's pieces are worked in antique variegated French silk ribbons, a gift from her aunt who was taught in Paris, France, during the late 1800s. Mrs. Vesper is a highly respected needlework artist and now lives with her husband in retirement. *(Photo: Sharon Risedorph)*

Below: A French beret has a new lease on life thanks to Elizabeth Moir's expertise with silk ribbon embroidery. Accompanying it are matching accessories; a hair bandeau, make-up compact, and eyeglass case. *(Photo: Elizabeth Moir)*

Right: Two exquisite Victorian needle cases decorated with delicate silk ribbon embroidery are displayed here with an ivory spindle, painted ivory pin holder, and antique embroidery scissors. *(Collection of Jean Fox. Photo: Britton's Photo)*

Below: A collection of silk ribbon embroidery from the late Victorian era. *(Courtesy of Kaethe Kliot. Photo: Sharon Risedorph)*

Middle right: Courtesy of the University of North Texas comes a black net cape by Givenchy. A tribute to bygone days, this cape proves that ribbon work is always in fashion. *(Photo: University of North Texas)*

Right: Detail of the Givenchy cape. *(Photo: University of North Texas)*

Left: Courtesy of the Metropolitan Museum of Art, New York City, a beautiful French dress from the third quarter of the 18th century. The petticoat is heavily decorated with fly fringe, floral sprays, and ruched ribbons. France is one of the few countries in which fashion and design were under the patronage of the royal court. It continues today under governmental patronage. *(Photo: Courtesy of Metropolitan Museum of Art)*

Below: Kaethe Kliot of Lacis in Berkeley, California, is a leading needlework expert as well as a collector. Here is an outlandish example of 1920s silk ribbon embroidery. The colors explode off the pale blue dress. *(Photo: Sharon Risedorph)*

Right: Detail of the dress at far left. *(Photo: Sharon Risedorph)*

21

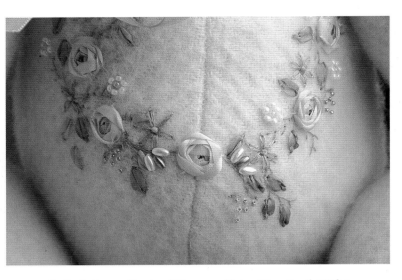

Left: Katheryn Sipple of Elemoore Vales, New South Wales, Australia, is a teddy bear expert who loves silk ribbon embroidery. Here, two wool teddies enjoy the company of a crazy-patch teddy on a wicker day bed in Anne's Glory Box Needlework Shop in New South Wales, Australia. Paws, ears, and tummies are beautifully embroidered with roses and daisies. The crazy-patch bear is from a *Family Circle* pattern and was made by Katheryn for her daughter's second birthday. *(Photo: Alan Carter)*

Above: Detail of teddy's tummy. *(Photo: Alan Carter)*

Left: While Judith was on her 1992 Australian tour, she met Pam Smith in her landscape class at the Cottage Crafts Shop in Camden, New South Wales. Pam was inspired by "The English Cottage and Garden" from *English Garden Embroidery* by Stafford Whiteaker. She produced this charming piece of mixed techniques using silk ribbon embroidery, yarns, lace fabrics, and netting. Pam is a quilting and embroidery teacher. *(Photo: Joy Klein, Illawong, N.S.W.)*

Right: Detail of Pam Smith's landscape. *(Photo: Joy Klein)*

Left: Marie Platt of Brisbane, Australia, is never without her raffia hat. She works at Ruth's Patchwork Shop for Ruth Stonely, a well-known contemporary quilt artist. Ruth embellished Marie's classic hat with large satin ribbon flowers, a beautiful addition for a beautiful girl. *(Photo: Judith Montano)*

Below left: Jan McCormick was in the landscape class in Camden, and she chose to design her rendition of an English painting ("Workers in a Field" by William Harford) that depicts fields of lavender. Jan has created a delightful piece using a variety of fabrics and lace, silk ribbon, yarns, beads, and doodads. *(Photo: Joy Klein)*

Below: Detail of Jan McCormick's Lavender Fields. *(Photo: Joy Klein)*

Left: French porcelain doll is ready for her trip with muff, hat, and steamer trunk. Remona Gibeson of Kansas City, Missouri, is a leading American doll maker. She adds silk ribbon embroidery to highlight doll dresses and accessories. Here, daisies and roses highlight a pleated dress. *(Photo: Sito Colon)*

Above: Specializing in silk ribbon embroidery and antique embroidery methods, Jean Fox of San Benito, Texas, is a delightful teacher. A beautiful black velvet vest shows off her talent. Flowers are ruched, gathered, and embroidered into wondrous shapes. *(Photo: Britton's Photo)*

Above: Carlton, New South Wales, Australia, is the home of English-born Heather Joynes. She is noted for her innovative use of silk ribbon embroidery. Florist's Window combines silk ribbon embroidery, floss and fabrics into a delightful picture. *(Courtesy Of Kangaroo Press. Photo: Heather Joynes)*

PHOTO: BRITTON'S PHOTO

Jean Fox

Jean Fox proudly proclaims her pioneer heritage of San Benito in the Lower Rio Grande Valley of Texas. Her family pioneered in this area as farmers. Her maternal side came to avoid South Dakota winters and her paternal side to avoid the Mexican Revolution of 1916. She lives on the same block where she was born and has been there for 60 years!

Jean's first teacher was her maternal grandmother who guided her at the age of 6 while she pieced a dolly quilt. Her mother was very handy with a needle, and her interests ranged from clothes making to quilts, needlepoint, crochet, and knitting.

Jean credits her late husband with a motto she lives by "Give away all your ideas, only make room in your head for new ideas!" This generous lady gives away her time and enthusiasm also. She teaches crazy quilting in the neighborhood and credits her interest in silk ribbon embroidery to her search for antique sewing tools and textiles. She became aware of antique needlework techniques and endeavored to apply them to her work. She first used silk ribbons on needlepoint projects.

Jean is a retired teacher who enjoys life to the fullest. To be in one of her classes, whether for one hour or in an on-going monthly meeting, is a treat.

Jean now uses silk ribbon embroidery on crazy quilts, clothing, quilted wall hangings, and needlepoint. She laughs when asked about how she began working in silk ribbon embroidery. She says "My learning experience in silk ribbon embroidery includes an insatiable buying habit. When I'm in the city I buy many supplies as I have few resources in my area. When companions ask me why I am buying 'that' (hoping for a revelation of some future project), I have to admit it is probably for my 'estate sale,' for things bought 25 years ago are either still 'too good to

use' or a suitable use still hasn't shown up. My 'estate sale' is going to be so good I may come to it myself!"

Jean is an expert at the "antique" method of silk ribbon embroidery. Her classes are full of laughter, anecdotes, and needlework hints, and old-fashioned techniques are passed along with style and ease.

Remona Gibeson

Remona Gibeson of Kansas City, Missouri, is a well-known doll maker. I first came across her work in a national doll-making magazine and was drawn to the ribbon embroidery on a French dolly dress.

Remona is the author of *Victorian Ribbon Embroidery For Dolls* (see source guide), and after a pleasant phone conversation, I decided to include her in my profile for experts. My decision was made as much for her honesty as for her needlework skills.

PHOTO: SITO COLON

She laughingly admits to thinking she had discovered silk ribbon embroidery. Years ago, she came across silk ribbon and tried some embroidery stitches with it. Soon she was adding it to doll costumes and including it in doll classes. Now her French porcelain dolls always wear garments decorated with silk ribbon embroidery.

Remona was born in Lake City, Kansas, and at the age of 5, her grandmother taught her to make dresses for her dolls and chain crochet. She was raised in the country and she has always had a love for old things and history. Remona's father was a ranch hand in the Oklahoma and Missouri areas.

She has been active in the art of ceramics for more than 26 years, specializing in the reproduction of antique porcelain dolls for the last 19 years. Remona holds the award of Master Doll Maker. This no-nonsense lady has written articles for *The Doll Artisan* and many other magazines. She travels extensively as an international doll judge and teacher. Her seminars are specialty classes on French and German porcelain dolls, clothing, French hand sewing, and, of course, silk ribbon embroidery.

Remona's classes vary from a one-day class to extensive seminars. She travels nationally and internationally.

Heather Joynes

eather Joynes of Carlton, New South Wales, Australia, can be credited with being the forerunner of the current silk ribbon embroidery craze. In 1984 she found a 1900s needlework magazine which featured silk ribbon embroidery. While browsing through the magazine, she thought she could do something with the technique. Eight years and two books later she is still involved in finding new ways to use the technique. And there is another book in the pipeline!

Heather was born and raised in London, England. She went to elementary school in a convent and then to high school in Blackheath until the war started and she was evacuated to Tunbridge Wells. Her mother was an excellent seamstress and made Heather and her sisters clothing until they were in their teens. Her mother was her first teacher, and her first project was a sampler at the age of 7 at the convent school. Now Heather enjoys the full support of her husband who is also her best critic. She can depend on him for an honest opinion of her work.

Heather is an innovative stitcher who is not afraid to mix media. She uses many different types of ribbon in addition to silk, and there is always a lot of thread stitchery in her work. She often uses hand-dyed (painted on) fabric as a background.

Heather is the author of *Ribbon Embroidery* (1988); *Creative Ribbon Embroidery* (1989); and *Stitches For Embroidery* (1991). They are published by Kangaroo Press, Kenthurst, N.S.W., Australia. She has been featured in *The Australian Women's Weekly, Handmade* (Australia), the *New Castle Herald*, and *The Advertiser*.

Heather teaches all over Australia and New Zealand. Silk ribbon embroidery is her most popular class, although she teaches many other techniques. She is willing to teach internationally. Her classes are always two days and can be both project- and design-oriented. For beginning students, Heather starts off with a sampler of flowers and ends up with a project such as a needle case or a small picture.

Gloria McKinnon

ix owning the largest needlework shop in Australia with needlework teaching plus international travel, and you have Gloria McKinnon. She is a talented, hard-working woman who lives, eats, and sleeps the needlework business.

Gloria was raised on a farm at Clunes, New South Wales, Australia, where she was never allowed to say, "I'm bored," because there was always embroidery to do. Her mother and aunt were ardent stitchers and still are. Her mother was a professional dressmaker for friends and locals. She worked beautiful embroideries for her Glory Box (hope chest) and encouraged Gloria to do the same.

Gloria's first official teacher was a Mrs. Taylor in Clunes, and her first project was a pair of bloomers. She recalls her first embroidery project was a 6" x 8" ballerina in needlepoint.

Gloria and her husband own a large retail needlework store, "Anne's Glory Box" in Newcastle, New South Wales, Australia, which keeps her extremely busy. Gloria teaches part time. She first discovered silk ribbon embroidery in 1985 and has offered it as a class with well-known teachers and herself for years.

Gloria combines silk ribbon with painting to further embellish the picture. She also makes traditional pins or brooches to wear, pillows for the bedroom and pictures for the wall. Gloria now combines teaching and buying trips in the United States. She also teaches in Australia and New Zealand. Her classes are all project-oriented and last six hours.

Gloria is presently working on a book. She and her beautiful shop have been written up in *Handmade, Craft and Home, Craft and Decorating* (all Australian magazines) and *Sew Beautiful* (U.S.A.).

Kaye Pyke

Kaye Pyke is a breath of fresh air in the world of needlework. Completely self-taught, she has developed a style that is readily recognized as a Kaye Pyke design. Her book, *Kaye Pyke's Elegant Embroidery*, is a huge success, and silk ribbon embroidery has been raised to a new level. Kaye has recently produced a second book with her co-author Lynne Landy, *Kaye Pyke's Classic Cushions*. The success of her books has created workshops all over Australia, from coast to coast.

Kaye has always enjoyed embroidery, particularly the creative and color elements. Her mother was very artistic and embroidered in a traditional way but did not venture into creative work. Kaye started needlepoint when she was at home with two young children. After a time she was bored with the repetitive stitches, so with a piece of calico and leftover wool, she started making up her own stitches — and she has never stopped.

Kaye was born and raised in Melbourne, Australia (with brief periods in the Greek Islands and Florence), and still calls it home. She now lives with her daughter who is extremely supportive and understands Kaye's passion for embroidery.

Kaye became interested in silk ribbon embroidery six years ago and has developed her own techniques and

designs gradually through experimentation. She is not a traditionalist — although she uses many traditional techniques. She experiments with silk ribbon embroidery constantly, and it is just a small part of the embroidery skills that she enjoys teaching. She likes to use silk techniques to build up a design, incorporating silk or cotton stitches to make an overall texture.

Kaye loves teaching embroidery and finds it very satisfying because of the wide variety of people attending her classes. Sometimes she will have three generations from one family — grandmother, daughter, and granddaughter — attend. There are lots of laughs, and everyone has a story to tell. Kaye's workshops vary from one-day to full-weekend workshops. (She is very willing to travel internationally). All her workshops are project-oriented.

Kaye also owns a beautiful boutique, which stocks all types of ribbons, silks, cottons, wools, fabrics, and accessories — including her elegantly embroidered cushions.

Merrilyn Heazelwood

Merrilyn Heazelwood was born in Launceston, Tasmania, a beautiful farming area that is often called "Little England," with rolling hills and hedges outlining the lush pastures. Her mother and grandmother both had art backgrounds and along with other women relatives were competent needlewomen. They encouraged Merrilyn when she was a child so that by the age of 4, she was knitting and making doll clothes. At the young age of 23, she opened her first craft shop.

Merrilyn's natural ability to work many forms of embroidery and her many art lessons soon developed into a teaching ability and the creation of many original designs. She has encouraged her customers and students to extend their stitching skills by offering a wide range of classes.

Merrilyn was bitten by the silk ribbon bug seven years ago when she worked a design on a woolen sweater. After countless washings, the ribbonwork is still fresh and lovely, and Merrilyn receives compliments each time that she wears it. She has written a line of popular silk ribbon embroidery books titled *Spring Bulb Sampler, Fuchsias,* and *Roses*. A fourth book, *Cottage Garden*, will be published in the spring of 1994.

Completely self taught, Merrilyn is proud of her non-traditional and non-perfectionist approach. She states that she is a "lazy stitcher," but she produces a lot of finished pieces. She says, "Silk ribbon is a very forgiving medium, and the width of the ribbon does most of the work."

Merrilyn is an artist with the needle and teaches throughout Australia, New Zealand, and internationally. All of her classes are based on one- and two-day workshops featuring projects from her books, which offer clear, concise instructions for designs that are worked within a grid format.

Frances Vesper

To meet Frances Vesper is to meet a real lady. Born in San Francisco in 1906, the year of the great earthquake, she missed the fire as her family was staying with friends in San José.

Frances claims the California earthquakes follow her around. She was in the Santa Barbara and Long Beach area during the 1940s quake. She and her husband were living in a 12th-floor condominium when the 1989 quake hit the Bay area. They lost a great deal of crystal and china and had to walk down 12 flights to the sidewalk where 31 plate glass windows had shattered.

PHOTO: SHARON RISEDORPH

Mrs. Vesper learned silk ribbon embroidery from her Aunt Sarah Hamilton at the age of 7. Sarah had lived for two years in the 1890s in Paris, France. There she took classes in traditional silk ribbon embroidery.

Sarah was adored by her niece Frances and was a very kind and generous person. She became a nanny for two children of a wealthy family and was truly loved by this family becoming a second mother to the children. Sarah made many embroidered pieces for the children, such as travel cases and lingerie holders. She taught Frances to make small flat flowers such as forget-me-nots, violets, and roses using the beautiful shaded French silk ribbons.

Frances was an art major, and it shows in her beautiful needlework. She thinks the most important thing for silk ribbon embroidery is keen observation and a sketchbook.

For years Mr. Vesper grew orchids and had more than 850 varieties in his greenhouse. After retirement he gave them up, and Frances could see how much he missed them. Her answer to the problem was two orchid pillows. He chose the orchids — one slipper and one large open orchid in yellow and apricot. The designs were so beautiful that she was encouraged by a local needlework shop to make a pattern.

Just talking and being with Frances Vesper is like a trip to bygone days where life is more tranquil and the gentle arts important. She learned needlework from her English mother Mary Frances Hamilton, and with instruction from both mother and aunt, she has carried on the family tradition. Her graceful pieces of silk ribbon embroidery take the viewer back to the Victorian era.

Mrs. Vesper enjoys retirement with her husband, and she does not teach classes. Her time is spent enjoying new needlework projects.

Elizabeth Moir

Elizabeth Moir of Perth, Australia, is an artist with silk ribbon and a needle. As a child she was attracted to silk fabrics and ribbons. Fortunately for Elizabeth her great-aunt was a couturier dress designer, who allowed her to play with scraps of exotic fabrics and trim. Elizabeth spent hours playing with silk taffeta, water-wave taffeta, and silk chiffon. Her mother says it was the only thing that kept her quiet and amused as a child.

Elizabeth has always been a keen embroiderer and became interested in silk ribbon work five years ago while visiting a friend in Sydney. Now she works exclusively in silk.

Flowers are a constant theme for Elizabeth. The three-dimensional look of the embroidery allows her to capture all the blooms in her garden.

Elizabeth loves flowers so much that she and her partner Moira Ryan organize a Perth craft fair twice a year, called The Victorian Rose Fair. This nostalgic fair attracts thousands of visitors each year to enjoy and buy romantic arts, crafts, and gifts.

Elizabeth encourages her students to try silk ribbon embroidery because "I love the sheen of silk and the three-dimensional effect; it's also easy to learn and you get to see the results of your work very quickly."

Elizabeth is a popular local teacher who is in constant demand. She teaches nationally in Australia and just made her international debut at the International Quilt Festival in Houston, Texas. This elegant lady was stopped every few steps at the Quilt Festival as people admired her black beret festooned with silk flowers (see page 19). Everyone fortunate enough to take her classes agrees that Elizabeth Moir is an excellent teacher. Elizabeth teaches half-day and full-day classes. She is also prepared to teach seminars of two days and more.

PHOTO: COURTESY OF ELIZABETH MOIR

The Basics

'm not suggesting that you rush out and get a degree in art, but I am suggesting that you take the time to become more observant! If you're going to work with silk ribbon embroidery, you will want to explore the possibility of new designs and patterns. These are as close as your garden, the local nursery, flower catalogs, coloring books, etc. Here's how to get started.

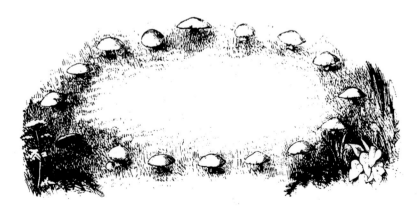

A Few Hints Before Starting

Sketchbook and paste-ups. Here is the author's sketchbook along with a few paste-ups, colored pens, and pencils.
(Photo: Judith Montano)

Open Your Eyes

1. Invest in a sketchbook. I like the big spiral binder kind. It is easy to carry around and to write in. It soon becomes a visual diary.

2. Use a pencil for fast sketches. You don't have to be an artist. Just get used to sketching in your book.

3. Colored pens and watercolor can help to record the colors and shades of the flowers and leaves.

4. When you come across pictures that show something you like, cut them out and paste them in your sketch book.

5. Work up samples, and paste them right into your book.

6. Use your eyes. Observe everything around you. I love to garden — it is therapy for me. During my lesson with Kay Ross in Brisbane, she gave me food for thought. She told me to look in my own garden for inspiration — and she was so right! There's nothing like being on your knees, hands in the dirt, nose to nose with your flowers!

7. In your sketchbook make notes about how many petals are in a flower — how many stamens. Notice if the shading begins light to dark, or vice versa. Make a note of the shape of the leaves, how many stems or branches there are. Relax and have fun with your sketchbook. It makes for great reading at the end of the year.

Shooting stars bring back many memories for me. They grew in wonderous profusion on the soft rolling foothills of my Alberta home.

Buffalo Bean

First came the crocus and then the Buffalo Bean. Such an odd name for such a pretty little lupin! They were tinged a pale yellow with feathery grey green leaves....

Wearability

1. Keep in mind at all times that silk ribbon embroidery is delicate and soft. It can not stand up to a lot of wear.

2. Decide right from the start whether it is to be washed or dry-cleaned and how much abuse it will receive.

3. From talking to the experts and from my own experience, I've found that wrapped, whipped, knotted, and braided stitches are much more durable, so I use these stitches on my clothing pieces and accessories.

4. Stitches such as the loop and plume stitches are very delicate and easily snagged — so these are used more in framed pieces and wall hangings.

5. Stitches that lie flat on the fabric with catch stitches (lazy daisy, fern stitch, cross stitch, fly stitch, etc.) wear quite well. You may have problems with some of these on loosely woven fabrics.

6. Straight stitches such as the Japanese ribbon stitch and the straight stitch buds wear well.

Blending of Background and Embroidery

1. Decide from the beginning on the background fabric. Does it lend itself to a casual or formal setting?

2. Make sure it does not detract from the embroidery in color or texture.

3. Consider the wearability of the fabric. How much wear and tear will it receive?

4. Check the weave to be sure it is sturdy enough to support the embroidery.

Color Choice

Decide on the tone or message you want to convey by choosing your colors.

1. For a soft, feminine look, choose pastel shades and a light, delicate background fabric. Use silk or cotton threads.

2. An antique or muted look can be achieved by using dusty tones — those colors, which are soft and grayed. Choose an appropriate background — moiré, silk taffeta, velvet — and keep the colors muted. Use silk threads.

3. A vibrant, contemporary look can be achieved with bright, jewel tones. Make the background fabric an equal color tone (black, fuchsia, etc.) so that it is strong enough to set off the jewel-tone ribbons. Use metallic threads for more sparkle.

Wearability — Samples of Pieces. The tighter the stitching, the more wearable a garment will be. Thus, the silk and tafetta ribbon flowers (*top left*), made by Wilanna Bristow in 1991, may not be the best choice for a garment. Lynn Bowden's fancy jacket (*top right*) will do nicely for evening wear. The detail from a wall hanging (*above*), made by Gloria McKinnon, will do well when used to brighten a room's walls but not its beds. And Wilanna Bristow's tiny sprays of lavender and violet flowers (*left*) are small and tight enough to be quite durable and wearable.

Mixing Media

1. Don't be afraid to mix silk ribbon embroidery with other embroidery techniques such as punch needle embroidery, crewelwork or cross stitch. Refer to *Crazy Quilt Odyssey*, and Julia Barton's *The Art of Embroidery* for ideas. (See the bibliography on page 125.)

2. Painting techniques should not be overlooked. Using dyes, acrylic paints, watercolors, gouache paints, or colored inks, a background can be painted directly onto the base fabrics. Don't overlook permanent-colored pens and fabric markers. These will give a softer look if the fabric is wet. (See page 122 for sources.)

Ribbon embroidery can be applied for dimension and texture. (Refer to the bibliography for further study on these techniques.) Have fun with blending these techniques into your original designs.

Close-up of Kaye Pyke's very feminine damask pillow with a monogram that is lovely in design and color.

Merrilyn Heazelwood's Fuchsias mixes media using both thread and ribbon and has a background that does not compete with the needlework. (*Courtesy of Merrilyn Heazelwood*)

Right: Painted background with ribbon work. An English cottage painted by the author is highlighted with silk ribbon flowers. The background is canvas. *(Photo: Judith Montano)*

Smocked and wrinkled work. A close-up of Desert Garden shows how silk ribbon holds the smocked and wrinkled fabric in place adding to the texture and interest. *(Photo: Judith Montano)*

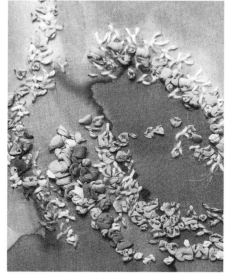

Left: Dyed fabric and embroidery. A dyed background by Roselind Morton of Brisbane, Australia, has been embellished by the author with silk ribbon. This piece is called Tide Pools. *(Photo: Judith Montano)*

Below: Crazy quilting and ribbon work. Crazy quilting forms the background on this weeping heart pendant by the author. The silk ribbon highlights the cigarette silk center. *(Photo: Judith Montano)*

Background Manipulation

Silk ribbon embroidery is lovely on a flat, subdued background, but it can be used on many types of backgrounds.

1. Dyed fabrics. Use hand-dyed fabric for a visual interest to the embroidery.
2. Crazy quilting and traditional quilting. Let the embroidery spill from one fabric piece to another.
3. Smocked or wrinkled fabrics. These are very effective for contemporary landscape work or free-form embroidery.

4. Traditional quilting lines. These thread lines can add visual interest to a background. Leaf designs or flowers can echo the ribbon flowers.

Threading Up the Ribbon

Silk ribbon is delicate and expensive, so you want to use a short length (12" to 16") and to use every possible inch of ribbon in the embroidery!

Traditional methods allow for a stitch that locks the ribbon into the eye of the needle and to make a soft knot at the end of the ribbon.

Needle Eye Lock: Thread the ribbon through the eye of the needle. Now pierce this end of the ribbon (directly in the center and ¼" from the end) with the point of the needle. Pull down on the long end of the ribbon, locking the ribbon firmly into the eye of the needle.

Soft Knot: Make the needle eye lock. Now grasp the end of the ribbon and form a circle with the end of the ribbon and the point of the needle (A). Pierce the end of the ribbon with a short running stitch (B). Pull the needle and ribbon through the running stitch to form the soft knot.

Ribbon Manipulation

You must learn to use the ribbon properly. If the ribbon is pulled too tight or it twists too much, it will just look like a heavy thread. Practice, and the following techniques will soon feel comfortable for you.

Keep the length of ribbon short (12" to 16"). It is easier to manipulate. Use your free thumb to hold the ribbon flat against the fabric. Most stitches depend on the ribbon being flat. Keep the thumb in place while you stitch and tighten the ribbon over the thumb. This will remove all the twists in the ribbon. A large needle or knitting stitch holder can be used instead of your thumb! This removes the twists before the stitch is completed.

Adjusting the Ribbon

Sometimes the ribbon folds up on itself as it passes through the fabric, and it has to be adjusted so the full width of the ribbon shows. Simply hold the ribbon flat under the free thumb and slide the needle under the ribbon, gently slide the needle back and forth (from thumb to needle hole in fabric). If this doesn't work, check the back to see if the ribbon is twisted near the stitch hole and adjust the ribbon.

Clothing Hints

Pattern Choice

hoose patterns that have flat areas for embroidery. Avoid pleats and darts. Make sure the garment has an area (yoke, collar, or front panel) that can showcase the silk ribbon embroidery.

Choose the pattern pieces to be embroidered and trace the outline in visible pencil onto the fabric. Cut out ½" (12mm) larger all the way around. (You can always cut down, but it's impossible to add on!) Transfer the embroidery pattern to the fabric, and work in a hoop.

If the design will spill over a seam, work up to the stitching line, sew the seam on the machine, press open, and return the piece to the hoop and embroider across the seam line, joining the two pieces of embroidery.

Once the embroidery is complete, cut the pattern piece to the correct size, and sew in place.

Design Placement

To make sure your silk ribbon embroidery is displayed to its best advantage, follow these ideas:

1. Make the design asymmetrical. Let the design flow over one shoulder, or down a sleeve. Don't make it regimented and a mirror image. Keep the design off center.
2. Don't "bullseye" the design.
3. Keep the design up and away from features you'd rather not point out (large hips, too ample bosom, etc.)
4. Display your embroidery where it can be seen (not under arms or in pleats!)
5. Always line the garment to cover the back of the stitches.

Cleaning

I've ruined too many projects by washing them, so I color-test all my ribbons, threads, and fabrics before I use them. A glass of warm, soapy water and a piece of the fabric dipped and draped over the side of the glass will soon let you know.

1. Children are naturally messy (as are most adults!) so it is wise to make their garments washable. I always wash the fabric in hot water and dry it at high heat before using it. What I get out of the dryer is what I use. Color-test the ribbons before using. Use buttons and beads that are colorfast, also.

2. Be sure to have formal wear and art garments that have taken hours of work dry-cleaned by an expert. It is well worth the expense. (Ask that your piece goes through the first solution of the day. A good dry cleaner changes solution every day.)

Purchased Clothing

There are so many off-the-rack garments that can be sparked up with silk ribbon embroidery.

1. Look for garments with linings that can be loosened — to allow a hoop to be slipped through.

2. Stitching on the yoke seams of shirts and blouses can be removed to accommodate the embroidery.

3. Ties can be highlighted with silk ribbon embroidery as can cloth belts, scarves, cloth purses, etc.

4. Sweaters are easy to decorate with silk ribbon. Weave the loose ends into the back stitches.

Finishing Up

After hours of embroidery and lots of hard work, it is time to finish the project. The finishing touches are every bit as important as the needlework. It is the difference between looking homemade or professional.

1. **Framed Work**. Work with a good framer, and you can't go wrong because the finished piece of embroidery is always cut ½" (12mm) larger than the opening of the mat board. Take this piece to your framer and choose a complementary paper mat. I prefer a double mat for many reasons. It enhances the finished look. It also gives me time to take the first mat home to insert the embroidery.

Purchased garment with ribbon work. Madeleine Montano and Sophie enjoy a quiet time on the back porch. Madeleine's T-shirt has been embroidered by the author to make it dressier and bright.
(Photo: Judith Montano)

a. Lay a bead of glue along the inside edge of the mat opening. Glue the finished piece in place. Use strong tape along the edges, and pull the fabric taut. Allow it to dry thoroughly.

b. Lay two or three layers of fleece behind the finished piece. The one closest to the finished piece is ¼" (6mm) larger than the opening — to make a smooth edge. The other one or two should be exactly the size of the mat opening.

c. Now glue the cardboard backing to the mat, wedging the fleece between. This will cause the finished piece to bulge slightly. Stack weights or books on top of mat. Allow to dry thoroughly.

d. Return to the framer and have the outside (second) mat glued in place.

e. The glass keeps everything clean and neat. In choosing a frame, make sure the glass never touches the embroidery work. Shadow box frames are great!

2. **Boxes, Metal Lids, Jewelry Linings**. There are so many different types, but nevertheless, most all are wooden or metal frames in which the finished embroidery is framed. It can be a metal lid on a crystal jar, the back of a brush, a wooden jewelry box, an oval brooch, etc.

a. Cut the finished piece to the size of the inside frame.

b. With Tacky Glue™, lay down a line of glue along the inside edge.

c. Glue the finished piece in place. Lay upside down so the finished piece rests on a flat surface.

Framed piece. Judith's grandfather is framed in a double mat. The piece is padded making the ribbon embroidery stand out. *(Photo: Judith Montano)*

Jewelry pieces and metal lids. An array of Framecraft pieces shows you how jewelry and porcelain bowls can be decorated with silk ribbon embroidery. *(Photo: Judith Montano)*

Left: Cloth box. Jean Fox made this charming cloth box and decorated it with a silk ribbon floral. *(Photo: Britton's Photo)*

Above: Kaye Pyke's pillow design made by Katheryn Sipple. *(Photo: Alan Carter)*

Below: Kaye Pyke pillow design.

d. Allow to dry thoroughly.

e. Now, pad the back with fleece and insert the backing. The fleece closest to the finished piece is ¼" (6mm) larger. Cut others to size of opening.

3. Accessories (Purses, Belts, Jewelry).

a. Keep the work backed with lightweight fleece.

b. Line your pieces with good-quality fabrics.

c. Finish all raw edges with cording.

d. Use iron-on Pellon™ on lining fabrics for extra body.

4. Pillows

a. Silk ribbon calls for opulent ruffles and lace, and wide, elaborate cording.

b. Make sure the lace or ruffle is large enough to balance the work.

c. Be sure the ruffle does not compete in color or size.

Tools & Materials

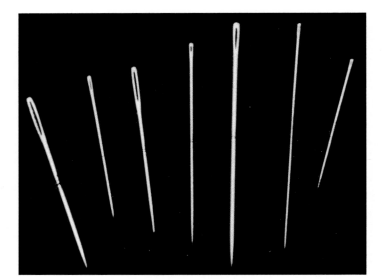

Variety of needles. Starting left to right are chenille, crewel, tapestry, straw, darner, and beading needles. You will need a variety of sizes of all of these needles for embroidery.
(Photo: Judith Montano)

 ou will find silk ribbon embroidery to be very exciting and rewarding. The stitches can be easily mastered and look more intricate than they are. Like any craft, it takes time and practice. Having the proper tools and materials on hand is half the battle.

Needles

 variety of needles is used for ribbon embroidery but the most often used will be chenille and tapestry needles. Crewel needles will be needed for the finer embroidery threads, and straw needles are wonderful for French and colonial knots. Beading needles are always useful for highlighting the flowers with beads.

When choosing a needle there are a few things to consider:

1. What kind of fabric are you working on?

2. Is the ribbon silk or satin?

3. Will the needle be piercing the fabric several times per stitch, or will it pass between the fabric and the ribbon?

4. How wide is the ribbon?

5. What type of stitch will you use?

Remember that the eye of the needle must be large enough and long enough to hold the ribbon and wide enough to make a large enough hole to allow the ribbon to pass through the background fabric without stress. The higher the number of the needle, the smaller the size of the needle. If the needle will be used to pull the ribbon between a previous stitch and the fabric, use a blunt needle. This way you won't snag the ribbon or fabric. If the fabric is heavy and an extremely tight weave, and if the stitch requires piercing the fabric a great deal, use a sharp point. (This becomes a matter of trial and error.)

1. **CHENILLE NEEDLE** — A large and long-eyed needle with a sharp point. Comes in sizes 18 to 24. Keep a good stock of all these sizes.

2. **CREWEL OR EMBROIDERY NEEDLE** — A sharp-pointed needle with a long narrow eye. Comes in sizes 1 to 10. Used originally for fine floss and yarn embroidery. Purchase an assorted packet of sizes 3 to 9.

3. **TAPESTRY NEEDLE** — A blunt-ended needle with a large eye. Used for cross stitch and needlepoint. Use in ribbon work to prevent snagging threads. Comes in sizes 13 to 26. Get an assortment of the most useful sizes — 18 to 24.

4. **STRAW NEEDLE** — Also known as a milliner's needle, it is long and narrow with the same thickness top to bottom. Wonderful for making French and colonial knots.

5. **DARNER** — A very long, large needle with a large eye. Can be a wool or cotton darner. Use for heavy threads and yarns or wide ribbons. Keep an assortment of sizes 14 to 18 on hand. Good for assembly work.

6. **BEADING NEEDLE** — A very thin, long needle with a small narrow eye. The beading sharps are much shorter and easier to use. I recommend a sharps #10.

More Tools

There are several things to make your ribbon embroidery easier. Such things as sharp scissors, stilettos, hoops, and thimbles might sound scary, but believe me, I've discovered through trial and error that they were made for a reason!

1. **STILETTO** — A sharp-pointed tool with a handle. This tool is used to pierce the fabric and make a hole large enough to accommodate the ribbon or yarn.

2. **SCISSORS** — Always keep a sharp pair of small, pointed embroidery scissors close at hand. The silk will snag if the scissors are dull. A pair of paper scissors should always be at hand as well as a large pair of fabric scissors.

3. **THIMBLES** — There are many types of thimbles and they vary from silver to plastic to leather. Try to get used to a thimble, especially when using the finer needles. If you have ever run a needle into your finger you'll learn to appreciate a thimble.

4. **HOOPS** — In ribbon embroidery, a hoop is very important. You will find it a bit awkward at first, but persevere. Make sure the hoop is small enough for both hands to reach the center area. Keep the fabric taut to prevent the stitches from drawing up the fabric. It also helps to keep the ribbon flat and the stitches even. When using plush fabrics (such as velvets) be careful that the hoop does not leave a permanent crease. I use a wooden hoop that has the inner ring wrapped in yarn. This works well on delicate fabrics like silks and voiles. Keep a variety of hoops on hand from 3" (7.5cm) to 8" (20cm). You'll find several different sizes mentioned with the project directions in this book. The clip style and plastic-lip hoop are also very useful. Just remember to remove your work from a hoop every time you put it away to prevent crushing the previous embroidery. I do a great deal of ribbon work on crazy-quilted pieces. Sometimes it is almost impossible to fit it in a hoop, but even three sides is better than nothing.

5. **KNITTING-STITCH HOLDER AND PLASTIC DARNING NEEDLES** — These are wonderful to use for loop stitches. Small and smooth — use instead of a round toothpick to hold loop in place

Stiletto, scissors, thimbles, hoops, and knitting-stitch holders are all helpful tools in silk ribbon embroidery. *(Photo: Judith Montano)*

Physical & Visual Aids

Learn to take care of your most valuable assets — your human tools — neck, hands and eyes.

1. To prevent shoulder fatigue, a simple thing like raising the height of your worktable will work wonders.

2. Your neck is under a great deal of strain while doing embroidery work. Never sit longer than an hour with your head bent forward. Set an alarm clock if you have to, and be sure to stand up and stretch.

3. Treating your hands to good lotions and a periodic manicure will prevent snags while working with silk ribbon. (Bag Balm is a faithful standard.)

4. Your eyes are even more important, so take extra care. There are many types of sewing lights and magnifying aids. I wear special half glasses, and they are a godsend. Ribbon embroidery is very fine and delicate. Using proper light (over the left shoulder for right-handers and the right for left-handers) plus some type of magnifier will work wonders.

Pens, Pencils, & Tracing Aids

ilk ribbon embroidery is rather free-form and when several people work the same pattern, the finished products will vary because of different tension and sense of proportion. Nevertheless, everyone starts out with a set design, and there are many aids to help transfer the design to the fabric.

1. **WATER ERASABLE PENS** — Use a very light hand with these pens. Make sure that all the marks are covered with embroidery. Erase with a wet cloth and cold water from the back.

2. **FADE-AWAY PENS** — Again, use a very light hand and be aware that the marks will fade after 24 hours. Works well if you can finish your project in a hurry.

3. **WHITE OR SILVER PENCIL** — Keep a sharp point and use on dark fabrics. I find these very successful.

4. **TRANSFER PENCILS** — Draw your pattern onto tracing paper with the transfer pencil. Lay the paper face down onto the fabric and iron on. This makes permanent transfer lines. Be aware that the pattern is reversed with this method.

5. **TRACING PAPER** — Good for transferring patterns from books or magazines. I like to save my pattern books and would rather transfer them to the fabric with tracing paper and transfer pencil.

6. **LIGHT BOX** — Another good way to transfer the pattern to your fabric. (I use a window in my sun room too!)

7. **NETTING** — Many Australian needleworkers use this method. They mark the dots and circles that represent the pattern onto the netting. The net is laid over the fabric, and the pattern is transferred with needlework pen or pencil. The netting is removed before stitching.

Pens, pencils, tracing paper, and color books will come in handy for ribbon work. These items are useful in transferring your designs. *(Photo: Judith Montano)*

Fabrics

he beauty of ribbon embroidery is that a great variety of fabrics can be used. Make sure the fabric is not too stiff because it will shred the ribbon. Ask yourself these questions when choosing a fabric:

1. Is the fabric appropriate for the subject matter?
2. Will it be easy to assemble?
3. Is it for casual or formal use?
4. Who is the intended recipient of this project?
5. How much wear and tear will it receive?

1. **PLUSH, VELVETS, AND WOOLS** — Work these fabrics with a large-eyed needle and a variety of wide silk ribbons and satins. Use stitches that will sit up on the fabric. Good for larger projects such as clothing and accessories.

2. **COTTONS, POLYESTERS, LINENS, AND SHANTUNGS** — These are medium-weight fabrics, and all work well for ribbon work. Good for smaller projects such as boxes, small accessories, pictures, and jewelry.

3. **MOIRÉ, TAFFETA, SHOT TAFFETAS, AND SATINS** — Wonderful for fancy work such as wedding or formal accessories.

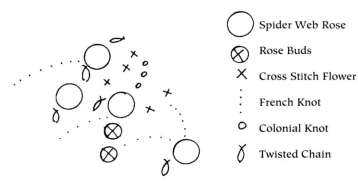

- ◯ Spider Web Rose
- ⊗ Rose Buds
- ✕ Cross Stitch Flower
- ⋮ French Knot
- ◦ Colonial Knot
- ✓ Twisted Chain

Variety of fabrics. Starting left to right are velvet, cotton, linen, shot taffeta, Thai silk, satin, moiré, loose-weave silk, light-weight polyester, light-weight silk, and organza. All can be used for silk ribbon work. *(Photo: Judith Montano)*

4. **LIGHT-WEIGHT SILKS, ORGANZAS, AND BATISTES** — Be very careful with these fabrics as they are very delicate. They may need a second layer underneath to stabilize them. Keep the threads and ribbons well concealed as they will show through such delicate fabrics.

5. **KNITS, LOOSELY WOVEN FABRICS** — These are very pretty when worked up. Some of the loose weaves may need a stable fabric on the back to hold the stitches in place (fine cottons or organzas).

6. **LEATHER AND ULTRA-SUEDE** — Have the stiletto ready— every hole must be punched. This is not for the faint of heart, and it is very tedious.

Threads

ilk ribbon work can be further highlighted with a variety of threads. Cotton floss, silk, metallics, and variegated fine yarns can be worked into stems, leaves, and berries. The centers of flowers can be worked with silk buttonhole twist or machine embroidery threads. Don't be afraid to try a variety of threads.

1. **NATESH** — a rayon thread with a wonderful sheen.

2. **PERLE COTTON** — a thick, twisted thread with a low lustre. Use #8 Perle for anchor stitches.

3. **SILK BUTTONHOLE TWIST** — a tightly woven thread that is equivalent to three strands of floss. This thread has a beautiful sheen. Great for branches, stems, and bullion knots.

4. **METALLICS** — shiny thread with a glitter. Wonderful for couching. Machine embroidery metallics are smoother and easier to work with. Use a short length.

5. **STRANDED EMBROIDERY FLOSS** — a six-stranded cotton that can be used in multiples or one strand at a time. Dull finish.

6. **BRAZILIAN EMBROIDERY THREAD** — a rayon twisted embroidery thread. This thread has a good sheen. Dampen with a cloth and use a short length as it tends to knot up.

7. **SILK OR RAYON MACHINE EMBROIDERY THREAD** — good for flower centers. Very fine and has a nice sheen.

8. **CREWEL YARN** — a fine three-stranded wool yarn that can be separated and used singly for embroidered stems and branches.

9. **MARLETT** — a very shiny, viscose thread. Comes in loose strands which can be separated for finer work.

10. **SOI D' ALGERE** — seven-stranded silk that can be separated or used as is.

11. **VER A SOI** — twisted silk thread similar to buttonhole twist.

12. **RIBBON FLOSS** — a shiny woven floss that can be used for heavier embroidery. Makes wonderful French and colonial knots.

Threads and yarns. From the top left are natesh, perle cotton, silk buttonhole twist, metallics, stranded embroidery floss, Brazilian embroidery thread, silk machine embroidery thread, crewel yarn, marlett, soi d'algere, ver a soi, and ribbon floss.
(Photo: Judith Montano)

Ribbons

ust the word ribbon conjures up beautiful visions: little girls with hair ribbons, mothers in dressing gowns decorated with silk ribbons, presents wrapped with satin ribbons. Ribbons are wonderful to work with! Silk ribbon embroidery, as the name implies, uses silk ribbon in various widths. It is a soft, pliable, bias ribbon. With care, satin ribbons and polyester ribbon can be used to highlight your works. The narrower the ribbon, the smaller the finished work.

1. **SILK RIBBON** — Once you've tried silk ribbon, you will never use any substitute. It is very pliable and soft. The bias silk ribbon retains its color and comes in a large range of colors. The most popular widths for embroidery are 2mm, 4mm and 7mm. It does come wider than this, but is difficult to find. There are many makers of silk ribbon, with the majority of them in Japan.

2. **SYNTHETIC RIBBON** — Looks like silk ribbon until you feel it. This ribbon comes in a limited range of colors (mostly bright, primary colors, but some come in softer shades) and will not behave like silk. Synthetic ribbon has more bounce to it and does not lie close to the fabric. Synthetic ribbon used for crochet and knitting is available at yarn shops and is worth investigating. It comes in a wider range of colors. Be aware that synthetic ribbon is coarser than silk and gives a heavier look to your project.

3. **SATIN (POLYESTER) RIBBON** — This heavier ribbon comes in a wide range of colors and widths —⅟₁₆" (1.5mm) to 3" (8cm). Use this ribbon for concertina roses, free-form flowers, and leaves. The very narrow ribbons can be couched for background fillers, stems, and branches. Use a stiletto if you choose to embroider with this ribbon.

4. **VELVET RIBBON** — Very plush and rich-looking, these ribbons are good for background. Lay them down first with couching or invisible stitches. Work silk ribbon embroidery over them (use a stiletto if you choose to embroider with these ribbons).

5. **SPARK ORGANDY** — This is a synthetic, see-through, sparkly ribbon and comes in a good variety of colors. Spark organdy is good for concertina roses and free-form flowers. The narrow (5mm) width is good for embroidery stitches. I recommend a large-eyed needle for this.

Ribbons. From top to bottom are silk ribbon, synthetic ribbon, two satin (polyester) ribbons, two velvet ribbons, and spark organdy.
(Photo: Judith Montano)

Highlights

on't be afraid to collage different techniques and materials together. Once you've finished the silk ribbon embroidery, it may look a bit dull or sparse. Beads, tiny buttons, or metal findings may be the *pièce de résistance*. Be sure to keep these highlights in proportion to your work.

1. **BEADS** — Small seed beads can add sparkle and visual beauty to silk ribbon work. Use them to fill in the center of flowers or to act as individual buds. Use Nymo™ beading thread for sewing them in place. It will not deteriorate with time or cleaning, and it is invisible.

2. **PEARLS AND LARGER BEADS** — There are so many varieties of pearl beads to choose from. Many of the old Venetian glass and jet beads would be good to add to your work. I use them as berries or as individual flowers.

3. **BUTTONS** — Keep the size of the buttons in proportion to the embroidery. Small mother-of-pearl buttons are very pretty with soft pastel work. Antique buttons are better with silk ribbon on velvet, etc.

4. **METAL FINDINGS** — Small brass and silver doodads come in a huge variety of shapes and subjects. Perhaps a little bee or a butterfly will add a special highlight to your creation. Birds or flower shapes could also be used. Have fun with these additions.

Storage of Tools & Materials

here is nothing more frustrating than the search for materials and tools when you are in the middle of a project. I speak from great experience! Here are a few suggestions from friends that I've used in my workroom and travels.

1. Store your ribbons and threads in see-through containers. Whether they are shoe boxes or plastic baggies on metal rings — get your materials out where they are readily available and visible.

2. Try to store your ribbons and threads by color if possible.

3. Keep your needles in a needle case according to size and use. Have one case in your workroom and one with the current project.

4. Keep a small pair of scissors with your current project(s) at all times.

Storage scene. Plastic boxes, baggies, and baskets are terrific aids in keeping yourself organized. Needle cases are invaluable for finding specific needles. *(Photo: Judith Montano)*

Beads, pearls, buttons, and doodads. Adding highlights to silk ribbon embroidery often creates just the right sparkle and energy to a design. Here are some examples of what you might find as you shop. *(Photo: Judith Montano)*

5. Pull the ribbons, thread, fabrics, and tools necessary for a project and keep them all in one container. I use my collection of Chinese sewing baskets for this. Use anything from plastic boxes to baskets to cloth carriers.

6. If you are traveling, a nylon casette-tape holder works beautifully as a needlework travel bag. The plastic sections will hold ribbon, thread, fabrics, and tools, plus the pocket will keep your project clean and safe. I found mine at a discount store, and they come in many sizes.

7. Store your current project ribbons and threads by color in ziplock baggies. Punch a hole in one corner of the bag and string onto a metal ring or tie with a ribbon. Write the color code on the ziplock bag with a permanent pen.

8. Purchase a small pillowcase or make one of calico (muslin). Store your unfinished projects in these little pillowcases. They keep your work clean and neat.

The Projects

he 12 projects on the following pages offer a wide variety of embroidery patterns. All of these silk ribbon embroidery patterns can be adapted to clothing, accessories, and jewelry. All of the patterns are actual size, and they are drawn in a realistic form. When a pattern calls for a "window" template, cut on the actual line of the pattern and remove the inside area so that a "window" or blank space is left for centering a fabric design or other element.

1. Have a Heart

ere is a charming heart pattern that adapts to three different projects, a whimsical doll, a keepsake ornament, and a sentimental pendant. The embroidery patterns are interchangeable.

Materials for all three patterns:

Chenille Needle   Embroidery Needle

Water-erasable   6" (15cm) hoop
  marker

Template plastic (for window template)

Have a Heart Doll

(Doll Size: 4" x 3¼" or 10cm x 8.5cm)

MATERIALS:

12" (30cm) square of   Small amount of batting
  even-weave fabric.   for stuffing.

Pink fabric paint for cheeks   Yarn for hair

Black and red embroidery   Silk Thread: two shades
  floss for eyes and lips   of green for stems

4mm silk ribbon: dark purple, lavender, blue, dark peach, light peach, and orange.

DIRECTIONS:

1. With water erasable pen, trace design and the two heart outlines (use a window template for this) onto the 12" (30cm) square.

2. Place fabric in a hoop and work the embroidery pattern.

3. Remove from hoop and cut on cutting line; cut a second one for backing.

ASSEMBLY FOR HAVE A HEART DOLL:

1. Cut two arms, two legs, and one head circle.

2. Place the two hearts right sides together and sew, using ⅛" (3mm) seam allowances. Leave arm, leg, and head openings. (Turn right side out through head opening.)

3. Sew up legs and arms, turn right side out, and stuff loosely with batting.

4. Run a basting stitch ¼" (6mm) from the edge of the head circle. Draw half way up and stuff firmly, making a ball shape. Draw up lightly, wind thread around the base and make a knot.

5. Place the arms and legs into the open slots and sew into place using the blind stitch.

6. Now stuff the heart shape through the head opening.

7. Place head into the head slot and sew into place.

8. Sew the eyes and lips with embroidery floss.

9. Paint the cheeks with fabric paint.

10. With a chenille needle sew the hair yarn into place. Keep it whimsical and wild.

11. With silk ribbon add a bow to her hair and tie bows around the wrists and ankles. Add one around her neck.

12. Remove water-erasable marker.

Heart Ornament

(Size: 3½" x 3¼" or 9cm x 8.5cm)

MATERIALS:

Three fancy buttons (to   9" (24cm) square of
  hold neck ribbon in place)   even-weave fabric

Small amount of batting   12" (30cm) of cording
  for stuffing

Silk thread: two shades of green   Fabric glue

4mm silk ribbon: three shades of green, three shades of peach, blue, yellow, rose.

DIRECTIONS:

1. Draw design and heart lines (one for front and another for the back) on the 9" (24cm) square with water-erasable pen.

2. Work the ribbon embroidery.

3. Remove from hoop and cut heart on the cutting line. Cut the second heart for backing.

ASSEMBLY FOR HAVE A HEART ORNAMENT:

1. Place right sides together and sew the heart pieces together using ⅛" (3mm) seam allowances. Leave the marked opening. Clip and turn right side out.

2. Stuff the heart with batting and sew the opening closed.

3. Starting in the heart crease lay a narrow bead of glue along the seamline. Smooth the cord into place, starting at the heart crease. Make a loop with the end of the cord. Allow to dry. Remove water-erasable marker.

4. Now with a matching thread sew the cord into place and take extra care to secure the loop in place.

5. Referring to the design, finish with loops of silk ribbon, forming a tassel.

Have a Heart Pendant

(Size: 4¼" x 3¼" or 10.3cm x 8.5cm)

MATERIALS:

6" (15cm) square of even-weave fabric
10" (25cm) square of pellon fleece
6" (15cm) square of muslin
6" (15cm) square of art board
6" (15cm) square of leather
30" (75cm) of cording for neck cord
14" (36cm) of cording for edging and tassel
Fabric glue
Darning needle and strong thread
Silk thread: medium green
4mm silk ribbon for Rose Bud Bower design:
   dark pink, light pink, green

DIRECTIONS:

1. Work the embroidery as above and cut on the cutting line. Remove water-erasable marker.
2. On the actual line, cut one muslin heart, three of fleece, one of art board, and one of leather.

ASSEMBLY FOR HAVE A HEART PENDANT:

1. Stack these cut hearts in order from the bottom; muslin, art board, three fleece, and on top the embroidered heart.

2. With strong thread and darning needle, whip stitch the heart over the fleece and art board, using the bottom muslin as an anchor. Sew around twice and on the second round, stitch deeper into the muslin to pull taut and even.

3. Glue leather backing to the heart. Let glue ooze out of the seam. Insert the tails of the neck cord between heart and leather, measuring out ½" (12mm) from the heart crease.

4. Twist cord, starting at the crease with the center of the 14" (36cm) cord.

5. Glue cord around the heart edges, tie a knot at the bottom for a tassel. Cut to desired length.

STITCH GUIDE:
For Rose Bud Bower design on the **HAVE A HEART PENDANT:**

Straight stitch

Rosette bud

French knot

Japanese ribbon stitch

Stem stitch

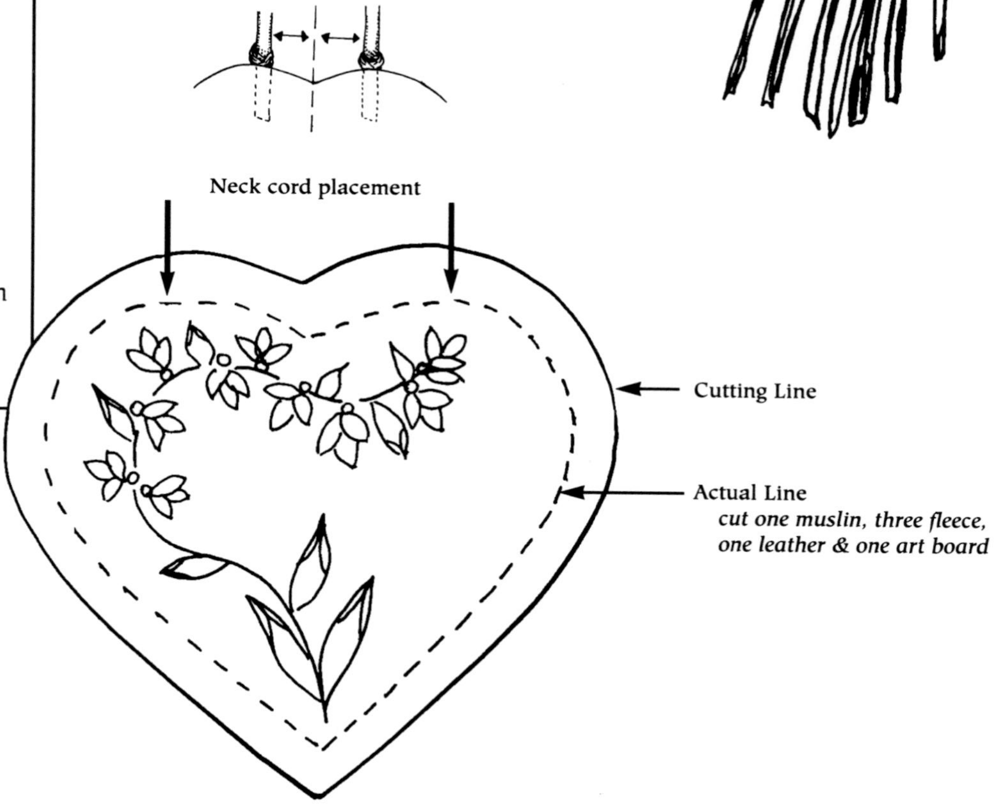

Neck cord placement

Cutting Line

Actual Line
cut one muslin, three fleece, one leather & one art board

44

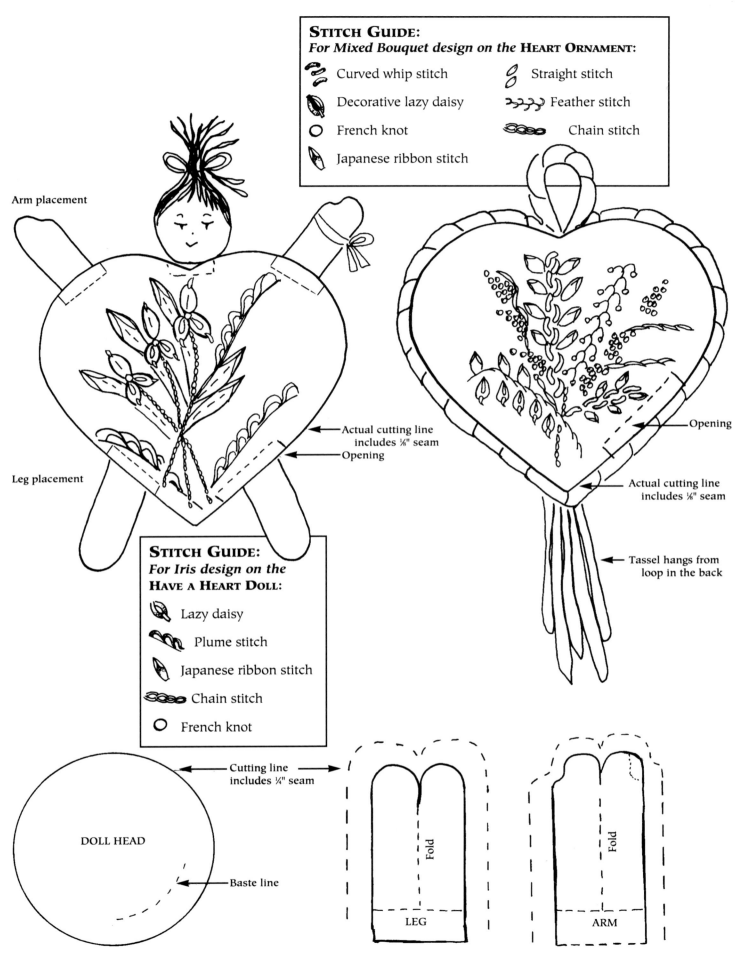

STITCH GUIDE:
For Mixed Bouquet design on the HEART ORNAMENT:

Curved whip stitch

Decorative lazy daisy

French knot

Japanese ribbon stitch

Straight stitch

Feather stitch

Chain stitch

Arm placement

Leg placement

Actual cutting line includes ⅛" seam

Opening

STITCH GUIDE:
For Iris design on the **HAVE A HEART DOLL:**

Lazy daisy

Plume stitch

Japanese ribbon stitch

Chain stitch

French knot

Opening

Actual cutting line includes ⅛" seam

Tassel hangs from loop in the back

Cutting line includes ¼" seam

DOLL HEAD

Baste line

Fold

LEG

Fold

ARM

45

2. Bow Ties

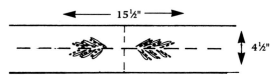

(Finished size: 2" x 5" or 5cm x 13cm)

ake the special men in you life a tie to remember. These elegant bow ties are perfect for weddings, proms, formal parties or just because! They are a conversation piece at every gathering.

MATERIALS:

¼ yard (24cm) of fancy fabric
   (moiré, cotton, velveteen, raw silk)
Velcro or snaps for fastening
Tapestry, embroidery, and chenille needles
6" (15cm) embroidery hoop
Marking pens (white or water erasable)
Silk thread or embroidery floss: green for stems

FOR WHEAT AND CHRISTMAS BERRY DESIGN:

4mm silk ribbon: four shades of rust to gold; three shades of red; green for leaves.

FOR SEAWEED DESIGN:

4mm silk ribbon: lavender,
   three shades of turquoise,
   three shades of dusty pink, green.
Silk thread or embroidery floss: turquoise.

DIRECTIONS:

1. Using the pattern on page 47, make a template for the bow tie (with a "window" for the embroidery area) to use for a pattern or mark the area directly on the fancy fabric. (The large rectangle is a 4½" x 15½" or 10.3cm x 38cm; the smaller rectangle is 2" x 5" or 5cm x 13cm and placed in the exact center of the larger one.)
2. Trace the design onto the embroidery area.
3. Work the chosen design in silk ribbon and threads.

ASSEMBLY FOR BOW TIES:

1. Cut out the 4½" x 15½" rectangle, making sure the embroidered area is centered.
2. Fold fabric so the design is on the inside.

3. Sew along the long edge in a ¼" (6mm) seam. Leave both ends open. Turn right side out.
4. Roll the seam to the center of the back and carefully press in place.

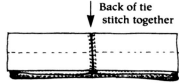

5. Turn in the open ends ¼" (6mm) and hand stitch closed.
6. Fold the tie into the center back on both sides. Stitch together.

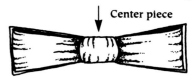

7. With thread or ribbon gather the center of the bow tie, and tie. (This is a temporary holder until you can sew the center piece in place.)
8. Sew center piece along the outside edge, turn right side out, and press into shape.
9. Roll the center piece around the center of the bow tie and sew in the back. This forms a cloth ring.

10. Fold neck band in half lengthwise and stitch ¼" (6mm) on long edge. Turn right side out. Turn raw edges to inside and blind stitch closed. Thread through the center piece in the back.
11. Add velcro or snaps to the ends of the neckband.

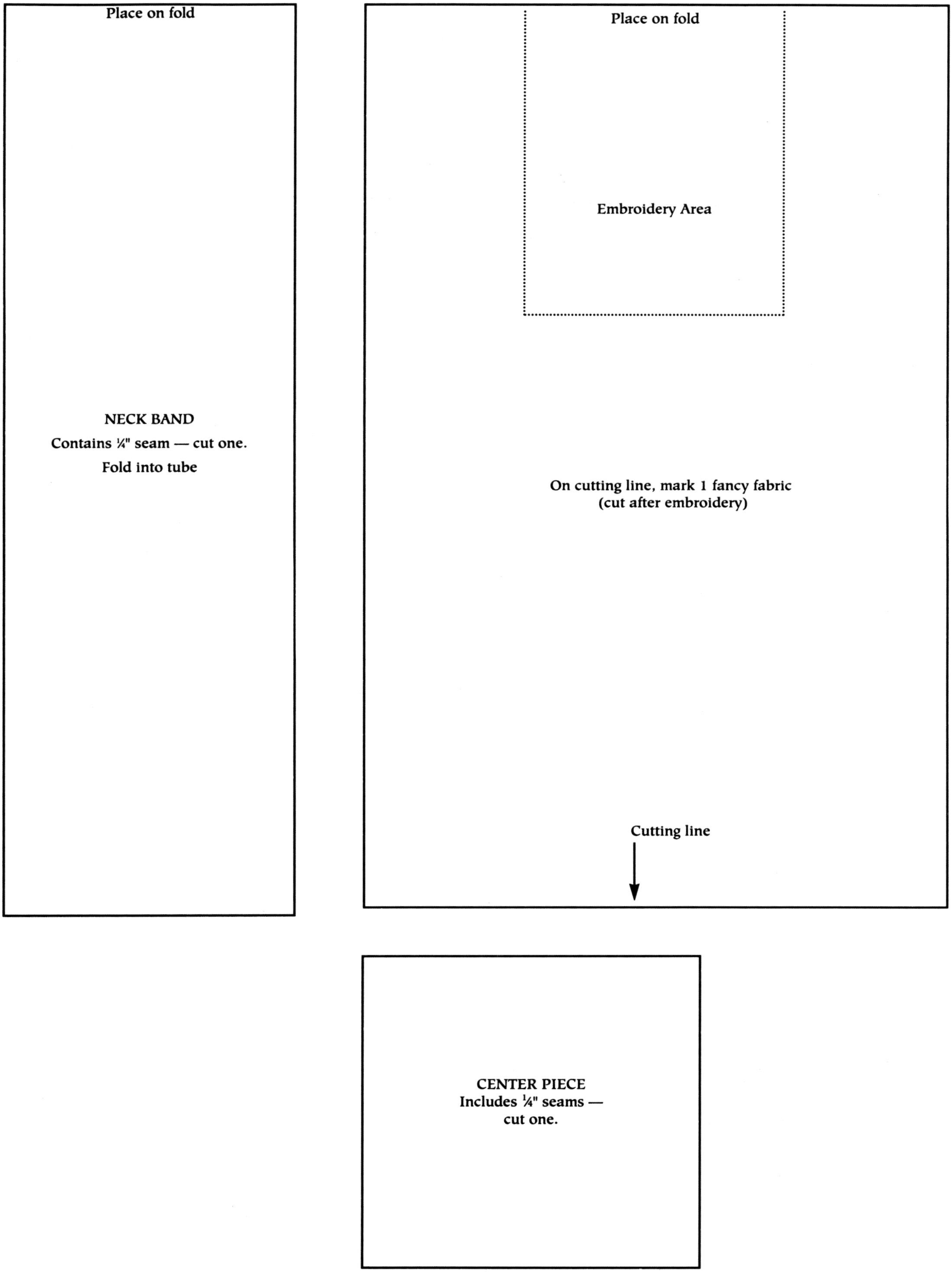
Place on fold
NECK BAND
Contains ¼" seam — cut one.
Fold into tube
Place on fold
Embroidery Area
On cutting line, mark 1 fancy fabric
(cut after embroidery)
Cutting line
CENTER PIECE
Includes ¼" seams —
cut one.

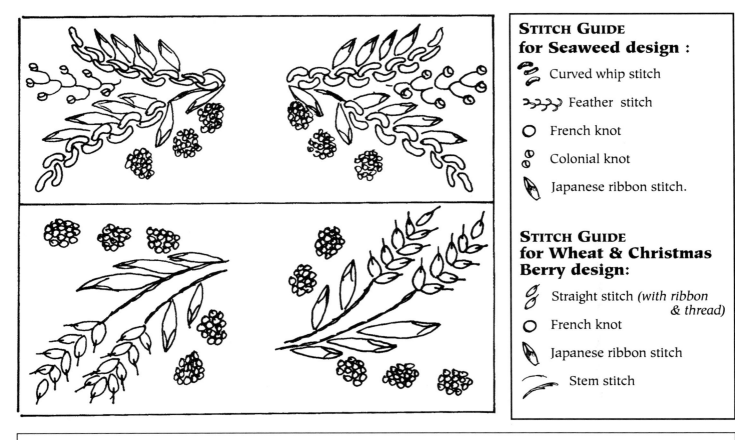

STITCH GUIDE
for Seaweed design :

∿ Curved whip stitch

ﻝﺯﺯﺯ Feather stitch

○ French knot

⊕ Colonial knot

◣ Japanese ribbon stitch.

STITCH GUIDE
for Wheat & Christmas Berry design:

◢ Straight stitch *(with ribbon & thread)*

○ French knot

◣ Japanese ribbon stitch

╱ Stem stitch

Crazy Quilting

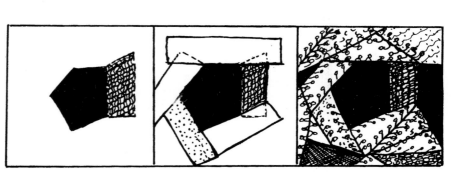

1. Cut a foundation fabric (preshrunk muslin or cotton outing) that is about 2" larger than the desired finished size.

2. From a dark fabric, cut a small center piece that has at least five angles. Pin it onto the foundation fabric at the approximate center.

3. Cut a wide rectangle and lay it against one side of the dark center, right sides together. Sew a ¼" seam. Flip the shape over to the right side and press the seam flat.

4. Cut a third wide rectangle and lay it along the next side of the dark center, right sides together, so that the new shape extends beyond both the center and the second previously sewn one. Sew a ¼" seam.

Trim any excess fabric from seam, flip the shape over to the right side, and press the seam flat.

5. Continue around until all angles of the center shape are stitched. Now cut new angles from the wide rectangle, forming various shapes and sizes. Then continue working around clockwise until the whole foundation is covered.

6. Once the piece is complete, press it on both front and back. Trim all edges even with the foundation edges.

7. Add embellishments — laces, decorative stitches, buttons, beads, and doodads — as desired to decorate the piece.

The Projects

Project No. 1. Have a Heart doll, ornament, and pendant. All are from the same heart shape with three different embroidery patterns — wonderful for gift giving. The circle pendant is by Tish Manley of Rogue River, Oregon. Tish was a student on the Caribbean Quilt Celebration '92. Judith offered a challenge to her students "to create a pendant using silk ribbon embroidery to commemorate the cruise and all the fun." Tish won the contest, and her piece certainly commemorates "Caribbean Memories." *(Photo: Bill O'Connor)*

Right: Projects Nos. 2 and 3. Shannon Gimble and Jason Montano
are all set for an evening on the town. The embroidered bow tie is perfect for formal and party wear and for the man who dares to be different. Here the young couple choose a corsage at Jo's Florals in Castle Rock, Colorado. The shell purse is a combination of crazy quilting and ribbon embroidery. Judith made this purse while traveling along the Great Barrier Reef of Australia. She loves to snorkel and is fascinated with the underwater life. This purse commemorates this time and emulates the coral and sea life. It is made entirely of Australian fabrics.
(Photo: Bill O'Connor)

Below: Purse detail. *(Photo: Bill O'Connor)*

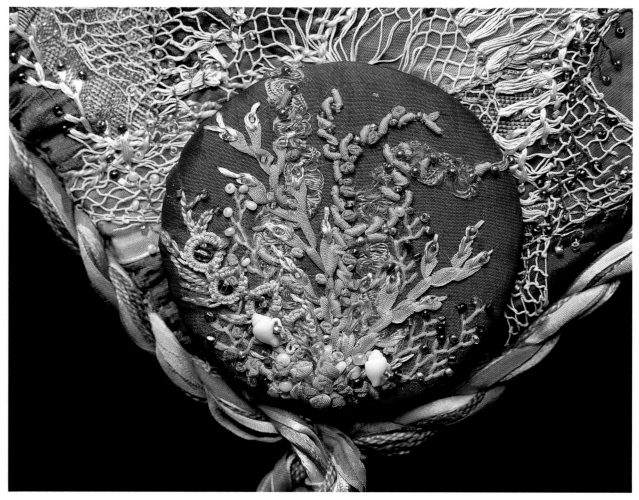

Project No. 4. Add a delicate and feminine touch to your dressing table or music box collection. These little moiré fabric packages contain a music box and potpourri! A beautiful, thoughtful gift for anyone. The pink moiré lid is for a crystal candy jar by Framecraft and filled with flowers from the author's garden. *(Photo: Bill O'Connor)*

Project No. 5. Frame the ones you love in elegant bouquets of silk ribbon flowers and moiré fabric. The small teal frame holds a photo of the author's Aunt Agnes at the age of 3. The larger frame holds an "adopted relative" Judith and her daughter Madeleine found in an antique shop. *(Photo: Bill O'Connor)*

Project No. 6. Ribbon and beaded brooches in a variety of shapes decorate a small nest of scrub oak leaves, liatrus, and pansies. Wonderful for gift giving, these charming brooches can be adapted to pendants and ornaments. The tassels are decorated with dentalia shells, beads, and doodads. *(Photo: Bill O'Connor)*

Project No. 7. Happy will be the bride who receives this delicate floral ring bearer's pillow. The ribbon for the rings is lightly tacked in place for later removal. Judith placed her favorite flowers on this special pillow: wild roses, forget-me-nots, daisies, and wisteria clusters. The moiré fabric is surrounded with cording and 18th-century French lace. *(Photo: Bill O'Connor)*

Project No. 8. The beauty of the Orient is captured in these charming little jewelry pouches. You will not be happy with just one. Use them for gift giving, potpourri, or to hold a special piece of jewelry. They can be made into a doll pouch that is charming and sweet. Judith used Thai silk for both pieces along with silk ribbon. *(Photo: Bill O'Connor)*

A velvet Victorian, Australian smoker's hat decorated with silk ribbon and threads rests on a Japanese jewelry box. The daisies are worked in silk ribbon, which sadly is disintegrating. Alongside the hat is a contemporary bow tie worked in a wheat pattern with Christmas berries on black moiré — a classic design for the discriminating man. (See Project No. 2 Bow Tie). *(Photo: Bill O'Connor)*

Project No. 9. At last! A way to preserve old photographs in an economical and elegant manner. The antique photographs are photocopied, and the photocopy is used to transfer the picture to fabric. Judith painted the cloth picture to give it a watercolor effect and then worked around the photo with silk ribbon embroidery. Here is a gathering of Judith's two children, Jason and Madeleine, at 3 years of age, Judith as a baby at 6 months, and another "adopted relative" known as Beatrice. Ribbon patterns are given for all three picture frames. *(Photo: Bill O'Connor)*

Above: Project No. 9. Judith has commemorated both her grandfathers, James A. Baker and Chet Van Winkle, with the Australian photo-transfer method and silk ribbon embroidery. Granddad Baker is surrounded by wheat sheaves and bramble berries, as he was a farmer. Grandfather Van Winkle, whom she never knew (he died when her mother was 14), is surrounded by forget-me-nots, cattails, and roses. (Patterns are in the project section.) *(Photo: Bill O'Connor)*

Right: Detail of baby picture. *(Photo: Bill O'Connor)*

Project No. 10. Garden Path is a study in various techniques. The fabric is painted with watercolor-type paints, and the garden path and wall are sketched with permanent pens. The flowers and textures are worked in silk ribbon and yarns. This is a challenging project that will give you hours of pleasure, and no two will ever be the same! *(Photo: Bill O'Connor)*

Project No. 11. All needles and scissors deserve a good home. What could be better or prettier than a Victorian reproduction of a needle case book and an embroidery scissors receptacle? Judith made these elegant little pieces from moiré fabric, silk and satin ribbons, and beads. They nestle among her collection of a Chinese embroidery booklet, a shell pincushion, a silks holder and an ivory malore. *(Photo: Bill O'Connor)*

Project No. 12. Wisteria brings back fond memories for the author. Judith used this flower to create a boudoir set of brush, mirror, and crystal bowl (all by Framecraft of Great Britain). The brush and mirror are topped with a bower of satin roses, baby's breath, and gladioli cascading down with delicate wisteria blossoms. The crystal bowl lid echoes the 1900s era with a chain stitch bower and embroidered wisteria trunk. *(Photo: Bill O'Connor)*

Zane Grey Trail — Judith has always specialized in mixing media. Here machine embroidery and scraps of silk fabrics provide a web of color for the circular scene that portrays the Zane Grey Trail, a special drive in New Mexico that epitomizes Grey's beautiful descriptions of landscapes. Silk fabric has been burned for the mountains. A mixed collection of ribbon, yarns, and threads provides texture. Semi-precious crystals and beads add sparkle and light. Silk ribbon provides color and depth. *(Photo: Bill O'Connor)*

Above: Michaelá Kovacs and Madeleine Montano in their embroidered party dresses. Michaelá's dress is white cotton with Chinese lace and embroidery insets (by Alison Rose for Dragonfly Company). Madeleine's dress is white damask (Made for Memories by Misty Lane). The author added the silk ribbon embroidery to give them a one-of-a-kind look. *(Photo: Bill O'Connor)*

Right: Detail of Madeleine's dress. *(Photo: Bill O'Connor)*

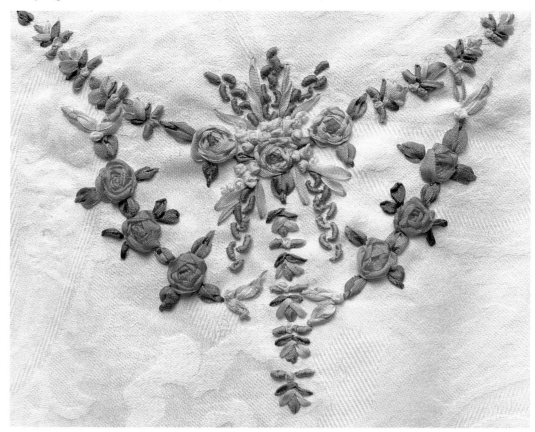

After finding four Victorian cigarette silks (by the Zira Company) in an antique shop, Judith worked them into elaborate hearts and mounted them on moiré fabrics. The top left hand queen is the Queen of Mesopotamia. Silk ribbon pansies, antique jet beads, and tatting surround this exotic queen. Peach and blue surround the Queen of Greece. Silk ribbon clusters, fresh water seed pearls, and ombre ribbon add a soft feminine touch. The Queen of Ireland calls for soft green and mauve. She is highlighted under a bower of silk ribbon roses, crystals, and antique sequin trim. Judith, Queen of the Hebrews, calls for purple and fuchsia. She is surrounded by antique glass bead trim, silk ribbon flowers, and tatting. *(Private collection. Photo: Bill O'Connor)*

3. Shell Purse and Seaweed Medallion

(Finished size: 9" x 9" or 24cm x 24cm)

ake this evening purse in Crazy quilting or use a fancy fabric and decorate it with more embroidery. It can be used with a shoulder strap or as a clutch purse. This elegant purse is a wonderful way to show off your collection of laces and doodads. As shown in the photograph, make a bow tie to match for the man in your life. Also, the Seaweed Medallion would make a beautiful pendant!

MATERIALS:

*Variety of fancy fabrics (solids, textures and prints)

⅓ yard (30cm) of fancy fabric for lining and backing

12" (30cm) square of fancy even-weave fabric for seaweed design

⅓ yard (30cm) of lightweight fleece

12" (30cm) ribbon floss or spark organdy

*14" (36cm) square of muslin

⅔ yard (60cm) iron-on pellon.

1½ yds. (137.4cm) cording for clutch purse

2¾ yds. (251cm) cording for shoulder style

12" (30cm) cording for circle piece (rattail)

Lace, buttons, doodads, shells

Beads, Nymo thread and #10 sharps beading needle, strong thread, and darning needle

6" (15cm) embroidery hoop

Variety of silk or cotton embroidery threads

Embroidery yarns

6" (15cm) square of art board

Chenille, tapestry, and embroidery needles

Velcro or large snap for closure

Fabric glue

White and water-erasable pens

SEAWEED DESIGN: 4mm silk ribbon: three shades of peach, three shades of dusty pink, two shades of teal, pale gold, and lavender.

* Omit the muslin and fancy fabrics if you do not use crazy quilting and cut a fancy front.

DIRECTIONS:

1. Make window templates. With opaque template cut the seashell shape for the purse. Cut on the actual line. Cut a circle template for the seaweed design. Cut on the actual line.

2. Cut two pellons, two linings, one backing, and four iron-on interfacings, all on the actual line for the purse shape.

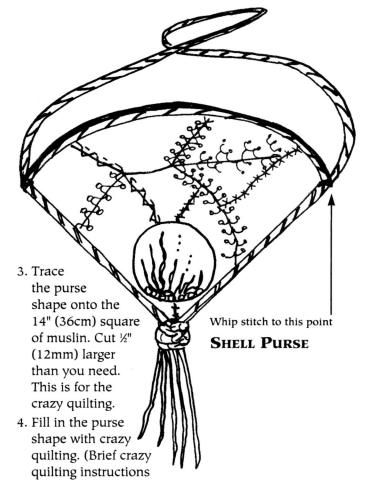

Whip stitch to this point

SHELL PURSE

3. Trace the purse shape onto the 14" (36cm) square of muslin. Cut ½" (12mm) larger than you need. This is for the crazy quilting.

4. Fill in the purse shape with crazy quilting. (Brief crazy quilting instructions are given on page 48. Refer to *Crazy Quilt Handbook* or *Crazy Quilt Odyssey* for more extensive instructions.) Press carefully.

5. Lay the purse window template on the crazy quilting. Find a pleasing pattern and draw an outline. Cut on this line.

6. Iron the iron-on interfacing to the wrong sides of the crazy quilt front, fancy back, and the two lining pieces.

7. Now lay down laces and ribbons on the crazy quilt front. Proceed to embroider all the seams with Victorian stitches.

8. Add beads and charms to finish the crazy quilting.

ASSEMBLY FOR SHELL PURSE:

1. Lay one fancy lining fabric piece flat right side up. Put the crazy quilt piece over it, right side down. Lay a piece of fleece on top. Use a pin to hold the pieces together.

2. With a ¼" (6mm) seam allowance, machine stitch around the shape; leave a 2" (5cm) opening at the side.

3. Trim the fleece ⅛" (3mm) from the seam to reduce bulk. Turn right side out and hand sew the opening closed.

4. Repeat for the back of the purse, layering the remaining backing right side up, lining right side down, and fleece. Press both finished sections.

5. Whip stitch front and back together, up to the points indicated on the pattern, leaving top opened.

6. Braid or twist the cords and tie the two ends together in a slip knot to form tassel.

7. Lay a narrow bead of glue along all edges and pin the cord in place around the purse. With the tassel hanging at the bottom, place cording up one side of purse, across one top edge of the purse opening. Repeat for other side, leaving excess cording for purse strap. Let dry and whip stitch the cording for extra security. Take extra care at top edges to secure the cords.

8. For the clutch purse, twist the cords until they are smooth and tight. Tie a knot at one end and use pins.

9. Lay a bead of glue along the top edges and sides. Start at the left top corner, laying the cord in place. Use pins.

10. Make a decorative loop at the bottom, continue up right side, and circle around purse opening. When coming up to the left corner, undo the knot, and tuck the cords under the twisted cords. Do the same at the right corner.

11. Let dry thoroughly and whip stitch in place. Take extra care at the corners to secure the raw ends.

Seaweed Medallion

DIRECTIONS:

1. Cut on the actual line three pellon fleece, one art board, and one muslin circle. Set aside until assembly.

2. Trace the circle on the 12" (30cm) square of fancy even-weave fabric, using a water erasable pen.

3. Trace the seaweed design onto the circle and put the fabric into a 6" (15cm) embroidery hoop.

4. Work the seaweed embroidery pattern. Use the ribbon floss or spark organdy seaweed. Take the 12" (30cm) strip of ribbon floss or spark organdy and tie a knot in one end.
Flare out the opposite end and pull up on a center thread. It will gather up on this thread in a ruching manner. Gather to the desired length and lay down in place. Tack down with Nymo thread.

5. Add beads, doodads, and shells until you are satisfied.

6. Cut out ½" (12mm) beyond the drawn circle. Remove water-erasable marker.

ASSEMBLY FOR SEAWEED MEDALLION:

1. Stack the circle pieces, from the bottom up: muslin, art board, three pellon circles, and the finished seaweed circle (cut ½" or 12mm larger).

2. Hold these pieces in your hand and with the darning needle and strong thread, sew around, bringing the seaweed fabric to the back. Use the muslin as your anchor. Sew around a second time, going deeper into the muslin to pull the embroidered seaweed circle taut over the art board and pellon.

3. Place a liberal amount of glue on the back of the medallion and glue into place on the front of the shell purse. Let it rest close to the edge and into the cording.

4. Allow to dry. Lay a thin bead of glue along the circle edge and lay down a rattail cord. Tuck in the raw edges.

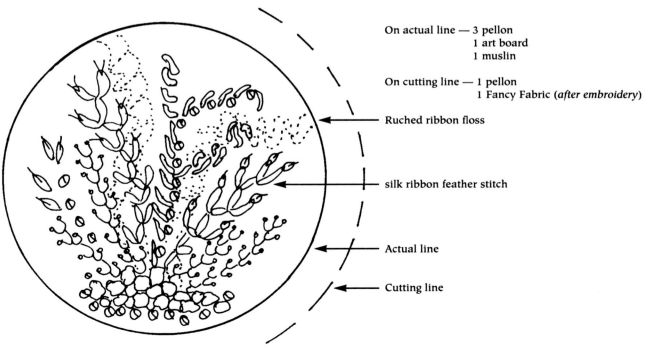

On actual line — 3 pellon
                  1 art board
                  1 muslin

On cutting line — 1 pellon
                  1 Fancy Fabric (*after embroidery*)

— Ruched ribbon floss

— silk ribbon feather stitch

— Actual line

— Cutting line

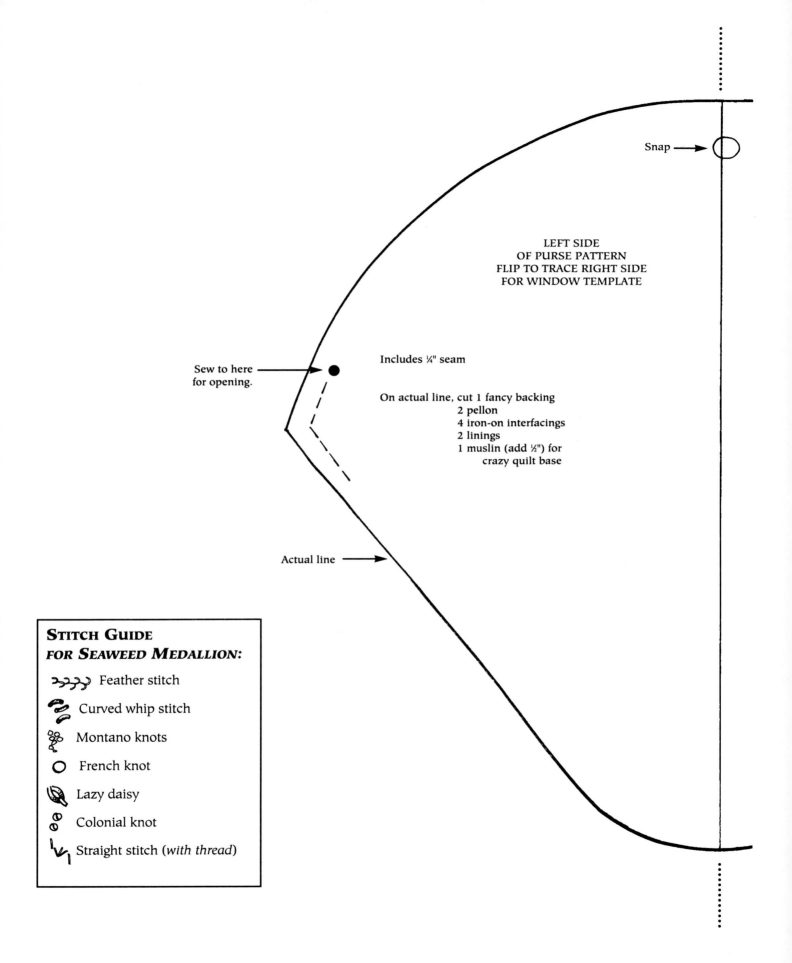

Snap →

LEFT SIDE
OF PURSE PATTERN
FLIP TO TRACE RIGHT SIDE
FOR WINDOW TEMPLATE

Sew to here → •
for opening.

Includes ¼" seam

On actual line, cut 1 fancy backing
2 pellon
4 iron-on interfacings
2 linings
1 muslin (add ½") for
crazy quilt base

Actual line →

STITCH GUIDE
FOR SEAWEED MEDALLION:

Feather stitch

Curved whip stitch

Montano knots

O French knot

Lazy daisy

Colonial knot

Straight stitch (*with thread*)

4. Music Sachets

(Size: 2½" x 4 ½" or 6.3cm x 10.3cm)

hese Victorian music sachets will appeal to women of all ages. Not only are they beautiful, but the sachets are functional, musical, and emit a perfumed scent. Wonderful for weddings, showers, and all-occasion gift giving. You will not be able to stop at just one.

MATERIALS:

½ yard (48cm) drapery-weight moiré or fancy fabric of choice

Large template plastic

6" (15cm) embroidery hoop

12" (30cm) picture framing wire

Small music box with removable key (can be found at most craft stores)

½ yd. (48cm) each of two fancy ribbons for bows

24" (60cm) cording

Potpourri or perfumed cotton ball

½ yd. (48cm) each of two ¼" (6mm) satin ribbons for concertina roses

Fabric Glue

Beads, Nymo thread, #10 sharps beading needle

Silk buttonhole twist: rust

4mm silk ribbons: gold, cream, blue, pink, lavender, four shades green

DIRECTIONS:

1. To make complete circle pattern on template plastic, trace ½ circle pattern given, flip over, and trace other half to form complete circle.

2. Use the template to cut two large circles from the fancy fabric.

3. Take the key out of the music box and set aside. Place the music box on its bottom in the center of one of the circles.

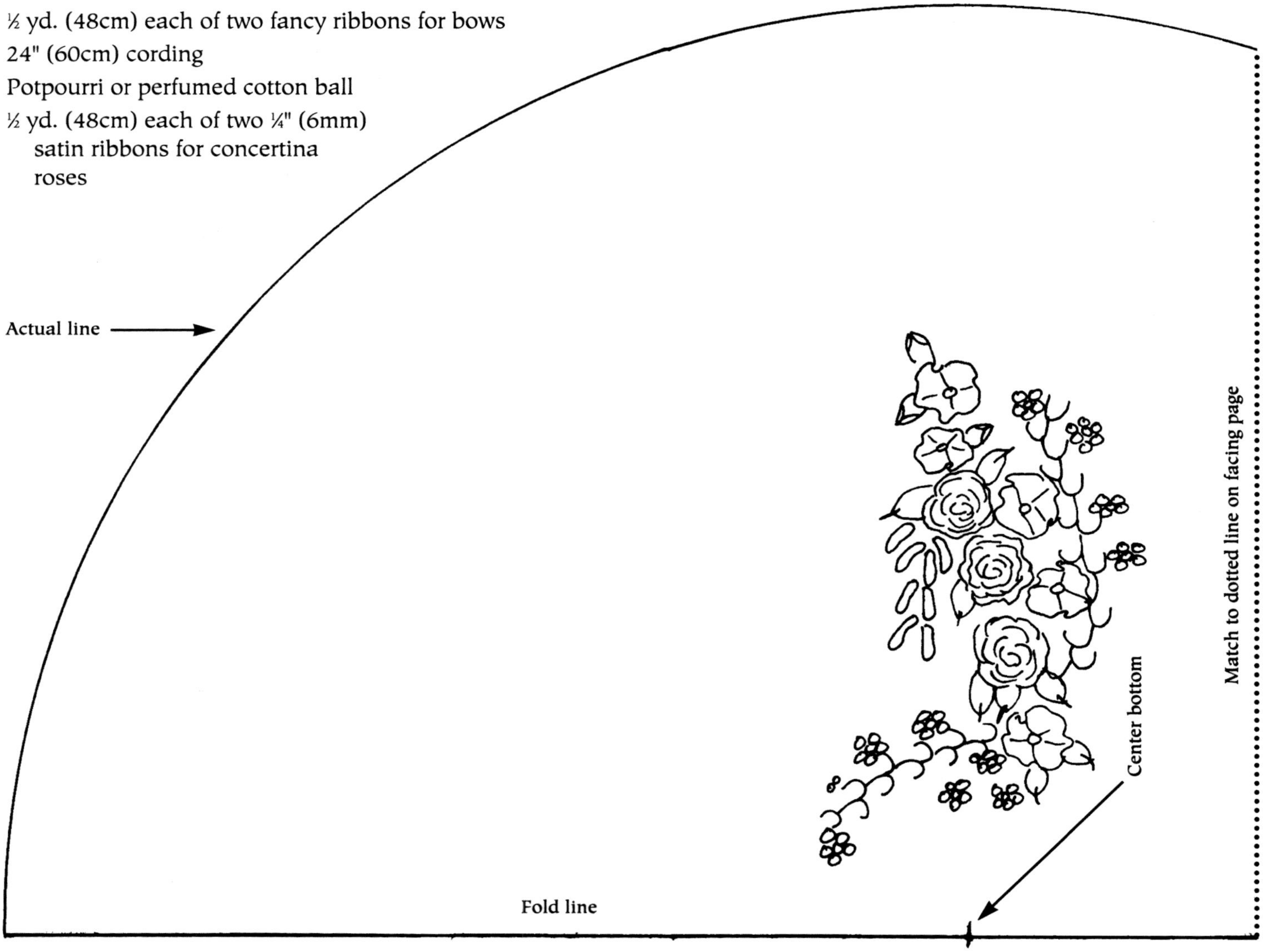

Actual line ⟶

Match to dotted line on facing page

Center bottom

Fold line

4. Gather the fabric up around the music box. With a water erasable pen, mark the outline of the front of the music box onto the fabric (on the right side). Music boxes vary in size and this is the only way to make sure the embroidery design will be centered properly on the front of the box.

5. Trace the flower pattern onto the circle. Draw it inside the outlines of the music box.

6. Place the fabric circle into a 6" (15cm) embroidery hoop and work the design.

ASSEMBLY FOR MUSIC SACHETS:

1. Lay the lining circle down with right side facing up. Place the embroidered circle face down on the lining circle. Pin together.

2. Sew all the way around the circle. Use a ¼" (6mm) seam.

3. In the center of the lining piece, cut a small slash about 2" (5cm) wide.

4. Pull the fabric through the 2" (5cm) slash to turn the circle right side out, and press the edges with a steam iron. You now have a perfect circle.

5. Place the music box in the center of the fabric circle and gather the fabric up around it. Make sure the embroidery is centered on the front of the music box.

6. Gather and tuck the excess along the sides.

7. Tuck into the top, a small amount of potpourri or a perfumed cotton ball.

8. With picture wire, wrap around the top, making sure it is very tight, and that the excess material folds and gathers in a pretty fashion.

9. Gather the two ½ yard (48cm) ribbons into folds. Place a bit of glue into the top center and push the ribbon folds into the center. Use a chopstick or stiletto for this.

10. Wrap the cording around the gathering point to cover the picture wire. Knot the ends to form a tassel.

11. Feel for the indentation of the music box keyhole in the back of the music box. With very sharp embroidery scissors, make a small hole (just big enough to push the screw end of the key into place) and insert the key. Wind into place.

On actual line, cut 2 fancy fabric

Match to dotted line on facing page

STITCH GUIDE for the MUSIC SACHET:

🌹 Concertina rose

⭕ French knot

🪡 Whip stitch

🌸 Free-form flowers

🌿 Lazy daisy

🍃 Japanese ribbon stitch

↝↝↝ Feather stitch

5. Victorian Moiré Frames

rame the ones you love in these elegant Victorian frames. Whether the photo is antique or contemporary, it will look wonderful in one of these frames. Choose fabric colors to complement the photo and surroundings.

MATERIALS FOR EACH SIZE:

⅓ yard (30cm) 44"-45" drapery-weight moiré or fancy fabric of choice for backing, lining, prop, and front

⅓ yard (30cm) 45" pellon fleece

1 sheet 20" x 30" (50cm x 75cm) medium-weight art board

1⅓ yards (122cm) fancy braid

Chenille, tapestry, and embroidery needles

6" (15cm) embroidery hoop

12" x 14" (30cm x 36cm) opaque template plastic

Fabric tacky glue and spray adhesive

Beads, Nymo thread, and #10 sharps beading needle

Water erasable marker and white marking pencil

LARGE FRAME BOUQUET MATERIALS:

Silk buttonhole twist or embroidery floss: medium green

¼" (6mm) satin ribbon: double-sided in cream, pale pink, off-white, and dusty pink

4mm silk ribbon: four shades of green, dark purple, medium purple, lavender, pink, four shades of peach, light turquoise, medium turquoise, gold, off-white, pale peach

SMALL FRAME FLORAL MATERIALS:

Silk buttonhole twist or embroidery floss: green and pale rust

4mm silk ribbon: four shades of purple (light to dark), light pink, medium pink, cream, pale peach, medium peach, four shades of green, light orange

DIRECTIONS:

1. Trace the prop and frame patterns onto template plastic using actual lines, and cut out for patterns.
2. On fancy fabric, mark two backs (without rectangle opening) and two props, and cut out ½" (12mm) beyond the marked lines.
3. On fleece, mark three fronts (with rectangle opening); cut two on marked line and the third ½" (12mm) beyond marked lines.
4. From art board, cut one front, two backs and two props. Cut on the line and cut out rectangle opening on front piece only.
5. Trace the frame pattern onto the fancy fabric for the front piece. Mark the rectangle opening, but do not cut out. Cut 2" (5cm) beyond the outer line.
6. Trace the embroidery design onto the front. Put into a hoop and work the floral design.
7. Upon completion, fill in with beads.
8. Remove from hoop and press gently from the back. Lay the piece face down into a terry towel.
9. Now, cut the outer edge down to ½" (12mm) seam allowance.
10. Cut out rectangle opening leaving a ½" (12mm) seam allowance.

ASSEMBLY FOR LARGE FRAME BOUQUET OR SMALL FRAME FLORAL:

1. Glue the three fleece pieces to the front of the art board frame; place the largest fleece on top. This insures a smooth edge.
2. Spray the top fleece with spray adhesive and glue the finished front to the padded art board front. Clip along inside and outside edges. Allow scissors to stop on the art board.
3. Fold the edges back and glue with tacky glue.
4. Spray one side of the art board back with spray adhesive. Lay the fancy fabric back, wrong side down, onto glued area. Clip the edges, fold to back, and glue with tacky glue.
5. Make two backs.
6. Glue the two backs firmly together. Weight with books until dry.
7. Score each art board prop on dashed line. Cover with fancy fabrics on unscored sides as you did for backs.
8. Glue together, leaving 1" (2.5cm) ends above scoring glue-free. Press tightly until dry.
9. Glue front and back pieces together along bottom and side edges; leave the top portion free (to insert the picture).
10. Decide on the tilt of the frame and glue the prop to the back. To ensure it always stays put, glue a fancy ribbon from the prop to the back of the frame.
11. Lay beads of glue along joined edges and cover with cording or braid. Tie knot on the side and let hang in a tassel form.

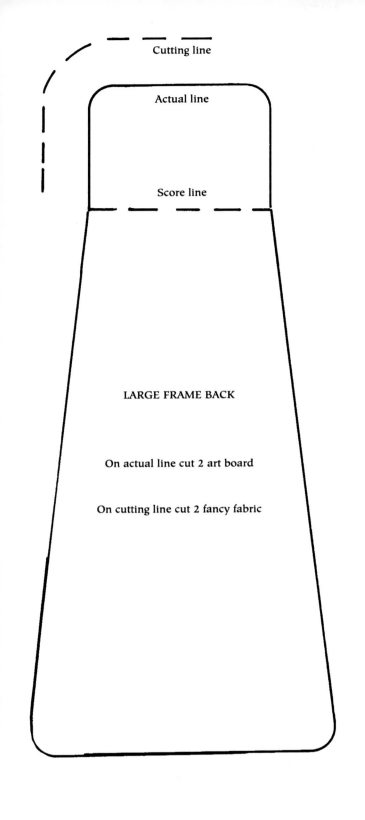

Cutting line

Actual line

Score line

LARGE FRAME BACK

On actual line cut 2 art board

On cutting line cut 2 fancy fabric

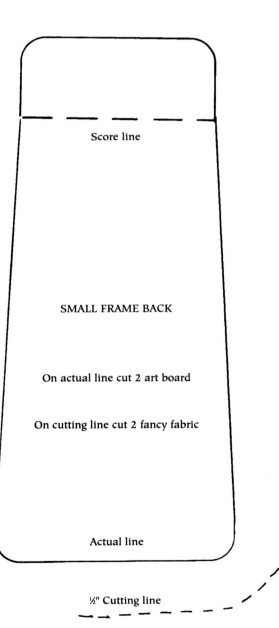

Score line

SMALL FRAME BACK

On actual line cut 2 art board

On cutting line cut 2 fancy fabric

Actual line

½" Cutting line

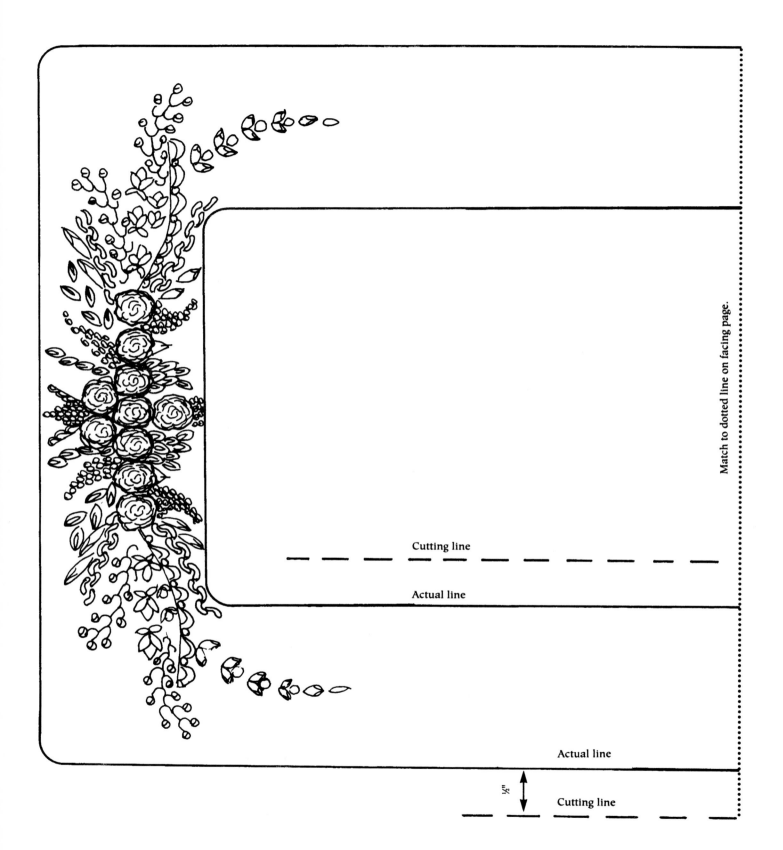

Cutting line

Actual line

Match to dotted line on facing page.

Actual line

½"

Cutting line

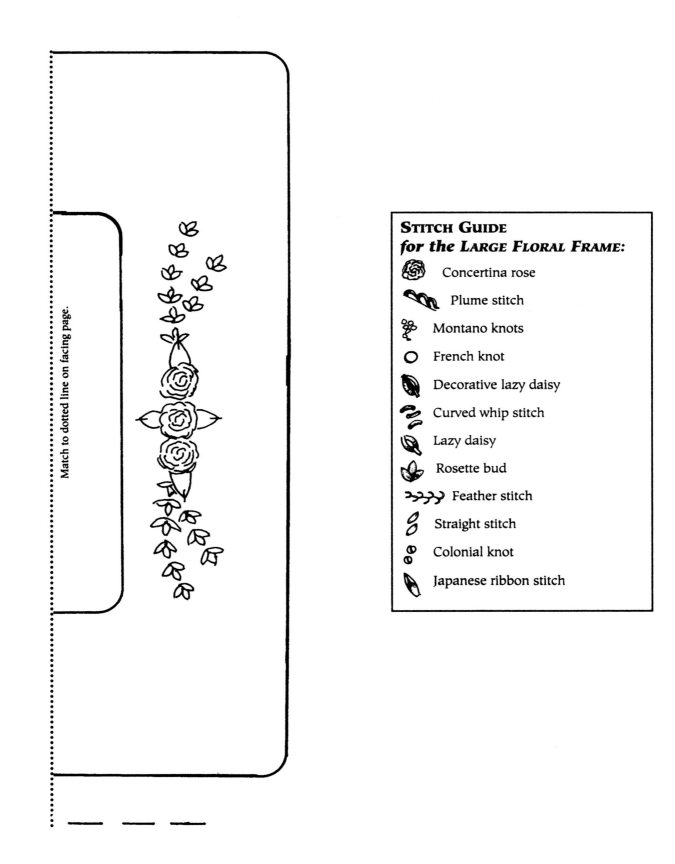

Match to dotted line on facing page.

STITCH GUIDE
for the LARGE FLORAL FRAME:

Concertina rose

Plume stitch

Montano knots

French knot

Decorative lazy daisy

Curved whip stitch

Lazy daisy

Rosette bud

Feather stitch

Straight stitch

Colonial knot

Japanese ribbon stitch

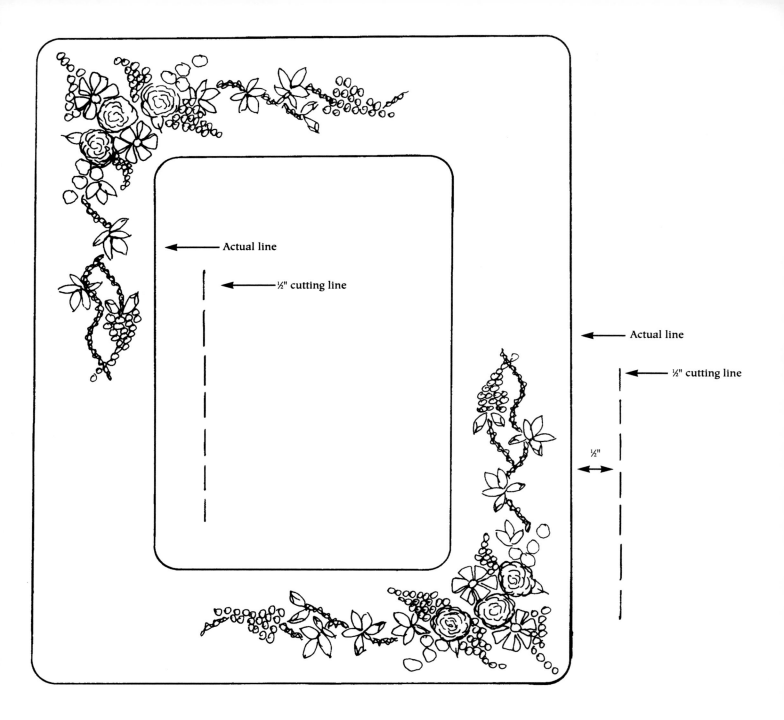

Actual line

½" cutting line

Actual line

½" cutting line

½"

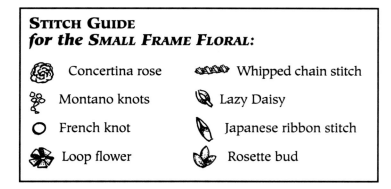

STITCH GUIDE
for the SMALL FRAME FLORAL:

Concertina rose   Whipped chain stitch

Montano knots   Lazy Daisy

French knot   Japanese ribbon stitch

Loop flower   Rosette bud

6. Ribbon Brooches

(Size: approximately 2" x 2½" or 5cm x 6.3cm)

 ou will have difficulty in deciding what shape and how many to make of these lovely little brooches. Here are five shapes, (oval, circle, heart, rectangle, and hexagon) to choose from. The designs also make up into lovely pendants and ornaments.

MATERIALS FOR ONE BROOCH:

6" (15cm) embroidery hoop

8" (20cm) square of moiré or fancy fabric

8" (20cm) square pellon fleece

4" (10cm) leather

4" (10cm) square of muslin

4" (10cm) square of art board

12" (30cm) square template plastic

Two 10" (25cm) pieces of ¼" (6mm) wide satin ribbon

Beads, beading needle (#10 sharps) and Nymo thread

Tacky Glue

Metal brooch

Chenille, tapestry, embroidery, and darning needles

Water erasable pen or white pencil

Strong thread for construction

Large beads and doodads for tassel

Three 15" (37.5cm) lengths of cording (such as rattail, silk ribbon, or yarn)

Rust silk thread for feather stitch

4mm silk ribbon: lavender, dark pink, light pink, two shades of turquoise, gold, four shades of green, cream

DIRECTIONS:

1. Trace all five shapes onto 12" (30cm) square of template plastic. Cut out and use as window templates.
2. Trace the shapes onto the fancy fabric with a water-erasable pen.
3. Trace the embroidery designs as well.
4. Place fabric in hoop. Follow the stitch guide, and work the embroidery patterns.
5. Highlight with beads.
6. Cut out embroidered shape ½" (12mm) larger than the actual pattern line. Set aside.
7. Cut one muslin, one art board, two fleeces, and one leather on the actual pattern line. Mark a third fleece ½" (12mm) larger and cut out.

ASSEMBLY FOR RIBBON BROOCH:

1. Starting from the bottom, stack muslin, art board, three fleece (with larger one on top), and embroidered piece.
2. With large needle and heavy thread, whip stitch the embroidered piece and larger fleece around to the back, anchoring into the muslin. Go around twice, pulling the finished piece taut the second time around.
3. Spread a heavy layer of glue across the back and affix the leather backing. Allow some glue to ooze out. Press lightly.
4. Twist the three cords and mark the center with a pin. Push the pin in the center top of the brooch. Lay cording in place along the edge in both directions.

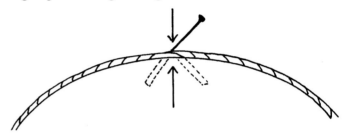

5. Tie in a tight knot at the center bottom to form a tassel.
6. Decorate the cords of the tassels with large beads, charms, and findings. Cut the tassel to a pleasing length.
7. Glue the metal brooch back to the leather back.
8. Glue a small rectangle of leather over the base of the metal brooch back for added security.

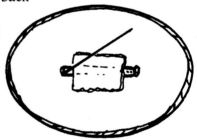

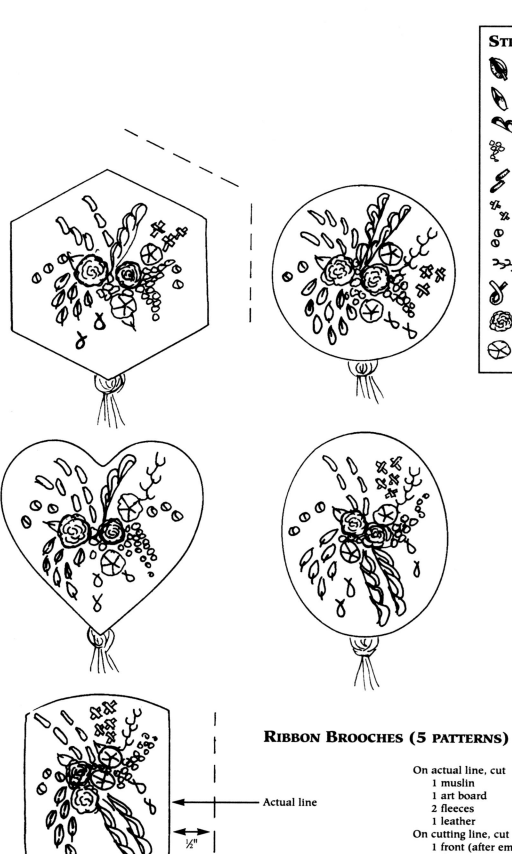

STITCH GUIDE:

- Decorative lazy daisy
- Japanese ribbon stitch
- Plume stitch
- Montano knots
- Whip stitch
- Cross stitch
- Colonial knot
- Feather stitch
- Detached twisted chain
- Concertina rose
- Spider web rose

Actual line

½"

Cutting line

RIBBON BROOCHES (5 PATTERNS)

On actual line, cut
  1 muslin
  1 art board
  2 fleeces
  1 leather
On cutting line, cut
  1 front (after embroidery)
  1 fleece

Add cutting line to all shapes

7. Ring Bearer's Pillow

(Finished size: 12" x 10" or 30cm x 25cm))

reate lifelong memories with this special, delicate pillow. Can be used as a ring bearer's pillow or as a shower gift or perhaps as a christening present. Whatever the occasion, it will highlight any room. Keep the colors soft and muted for a Victorian look.

MATERIALS:

⅓ yard (30cm) of cream-colored moiré, satin, or silk fabric

Chenille, tapestry, and embroidery needles

Water erasable pen

6" (15cm) embroidery hoop

Tacky glue

14" x 14" (36cm x 36cm) template plastic

⅓ yard (30cm) cotton muslin for liner

Small bag of polyester batting

40" (100cm) of ruffled lace (or 80" x 7" or 200cm x 18cm fancy fabric for a fabric ruffle)

40" (100cm) satin cording for cording insert

Two small metal safety pins

20" (50cm) cream, double-sided satin ribbon (to tie rings to pillow)

Silk buttonhole twist or embroidery floss: three shades of green

7mm silk ribbon: medium pink

4mm silk ribbon: two shades pale peach, medium turquoise blue, gold, four shades of lavender, medium pink, four shades of green

DIRECTIONS:

1. Cut heart shape out of template plastic. This will be a permanent pattern.
2. Trace the heart shape with water erasable pen onto the fabric. Use a light hand. This line includes a ¼" (6mm) seam allowance. Trace two hearts (one for front and one for the back).
3. Cut the heart shape for the back and set aside.
4. Leave the front heart shape on the square of fabric. Trace the embroidery design onto the heart.
5. Work the stems first in silk or cotton floss. Next add the silk flowers and leaves.
6. Now cut the heart shape on the cutting line.
7. Press very carefully on the back of the work (into a terrycloth towel) taking extra care not to smash the loop roses.

ASSEMBLY FOR RING BEARER'S PILLOW:

1. Pin the lace or fabric ruffle in place and baste by machine or hand onto the front of the finished piece. Pin the basted ruffle down so it stays in place.
2. Lay the backing face down on the ruffled embroidered piece. Pin together. Sew with a ¼" (6mm) seam line, leaving a 3½" (9cm) opening for the pillow insert. Remove pins, turn right side out, and remove ruffle pins.
3. For pillow insert, trace the heart design onto the muslin (folded double) and cut two hearts.
4. Sew together with a ¼" (6mm) seam line and leave a small opening. Turn right side out and press.
5. Stuff with polyester batting. Sew the opening closed, and insert this muslin pillow into the 3½" (9cm) opening of the fancy embroidered pillow.
6. Sew the 3½" (9cm) opening closed with matching thread.
7. Glue cording in place along edge.
8. If this is to be a ring bearer's pillow, cut two lengths of satin ribbon. Use small safety pins to position ribbons. Tie the rings in loose bows — no knots!!

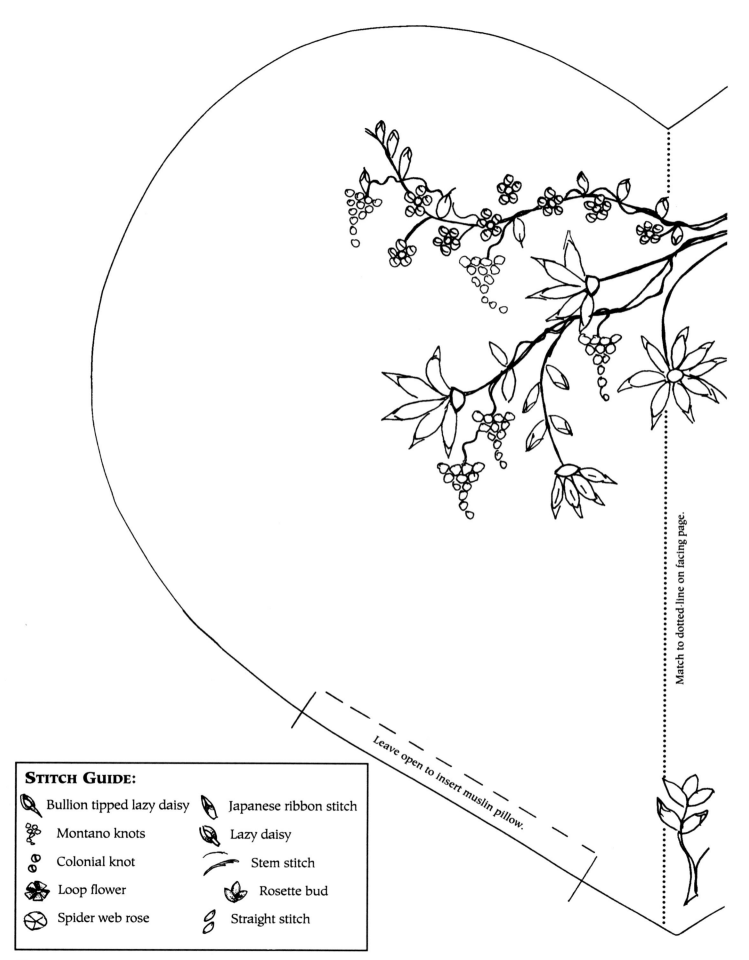

Leave open to insert muslin pillow.

Match to dotted-line on facing page.

STITCH GUIDE:

Bullion tipped lazy daisy

Montano knots

Colonial knot

Loop flower

Spider web rose

Japanese ribbon stitch

Lazy daisy

Stem stitch

Rosette bud

Straight stitch

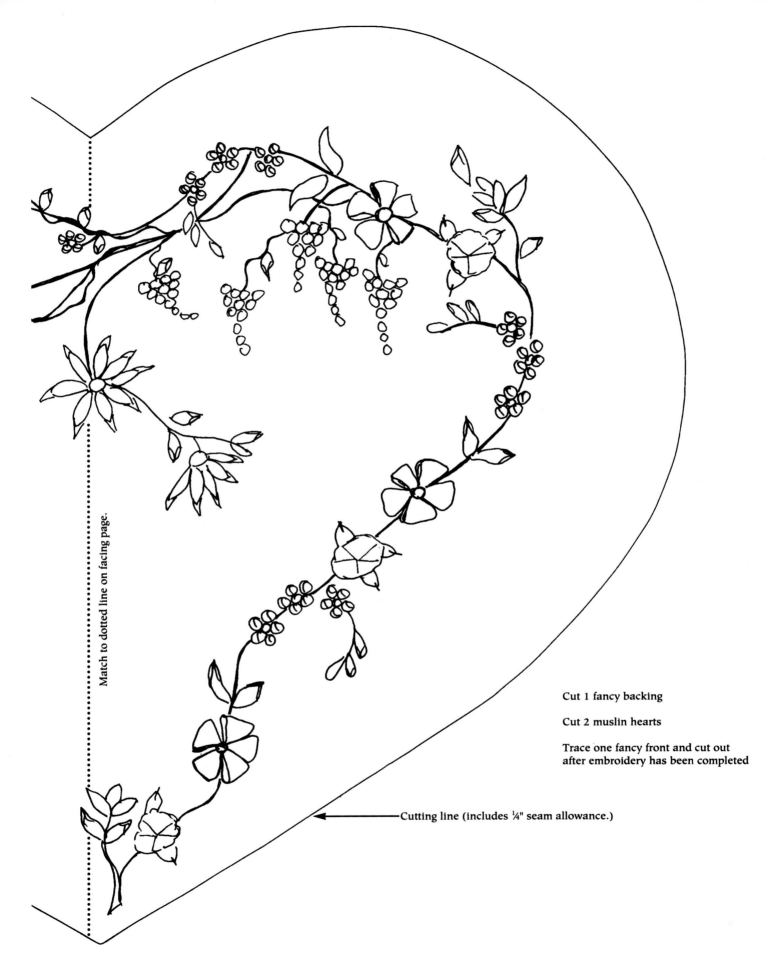

Match to dotted line on facing page.

Cut 1 fancy backing

Cut 2 muslin hearts

Trace one fancy front and cut out
after embroidery has been completed

Cutting line (includes ¼" seam allowance.)

8. Oriental Pouches

(Finished size: 3" x 5¼" or 8cm x 13.1cm)

 ast meets West with these elegant little jewelry and gift pouches. Worked in jewel-tone silk fabrics, they look rich and artistic. The little doll pouch is a conversation piece as well. Work them in an array of colors for gift giving and storage of precious keepsakes.

MATERIALS FOR DOLL POUCH:

8" x 12" (20cm x 30cm) rectangle of silk fabric
Two 12" (30cm) lengths of 4mm silk ribbon for drawstring

* For doll's head: 2" (5cm) circle of flesh-colored silk.
* Permanent marking pens: black and red
* Small ¾" (18mm) diameter styrofoam ball or wooden bead
* 2 yds. (183cm) black 4mm silk ribbon for hair
Chenille, embroidery, and tapestry needles
6" (15cm) embroidery hoop
Silk buttonhole twist or floss: three shades of green
Silk thread to match ribbon for woodland fern design.
For fern design: 4mm silk ribbon: three shades of green,

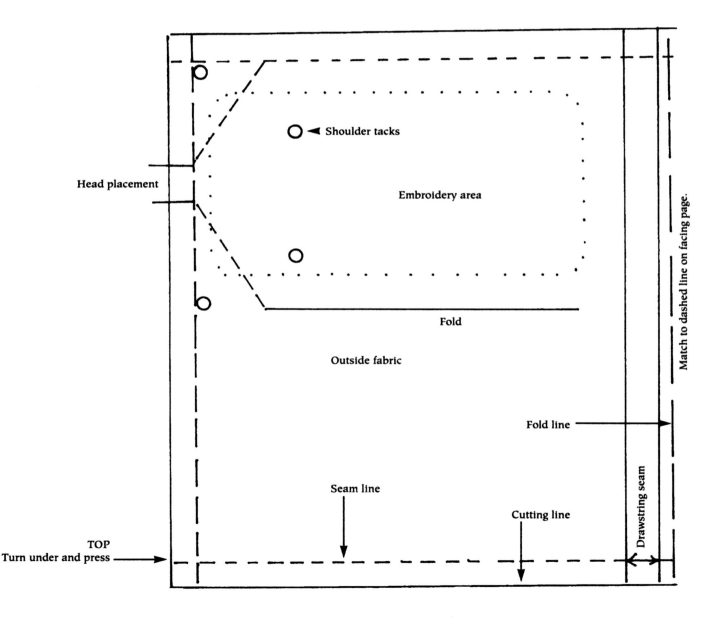

three shades of orange, pale blue, gold, cream

* For doll design: 4mm silk ribbon: three shades of orange, turquoise, gold, green

* For regular pouch, eliminate the doll's head, materials, and instructions.

DIRECTIONS:

1. Trace the outline of the pouch with lining onto the silk fabric.

2. Mark area for embroidery with water erasable pen or white pencil. Work the embroidery with 4mm silk ribbon and threads.

3. For Doll Pouch, cut the 2" (5cm) circle from the flesh-colored silk.

4. Run a basting thread ¼" (6mm) from the edge. Pull up, insert the styrofoam ball or bead, draw up tightly, and wrap the neck tightly. Tie off with a slip knot.

gathering line

5. Mark the eyes and lips with marking pens. With the black silk ribbon and a chenille needle, fill in the head area, taking long, flat filler stitches from front to back. Once it is filled in, pull several loops of ribbon through the back to form a long length of hair. Tie in place with a colorful ribbon.

6. Use regular blusher to rouge in cheeks.

7. For the regular pouch, omit steps 3-6.

ASSEMBLY FOR ORIENTAL POUCHES:

1. Fold the rectangular piece in a long tube with the needlework on the inside.

2. Sew a ¼" (6mm) seam on the long side. Press seam open and turn right side out.

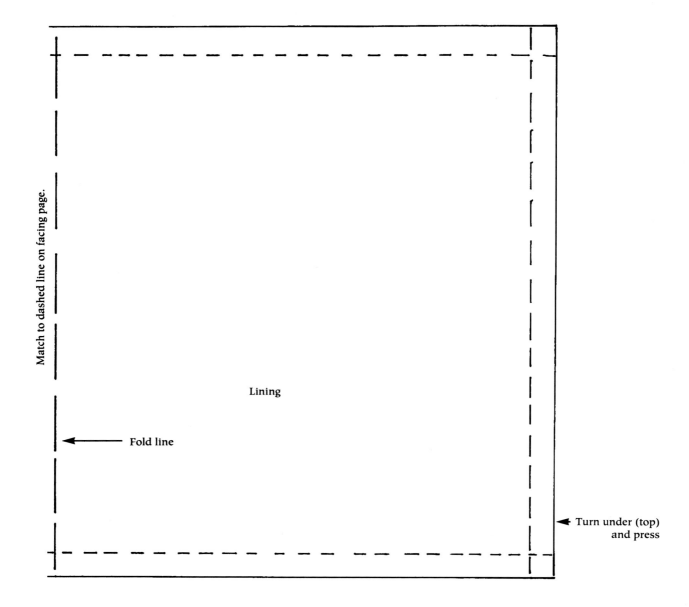

Match to dashed line on facing page.

Lining

← Fold line

◄ Turn under (top) and press

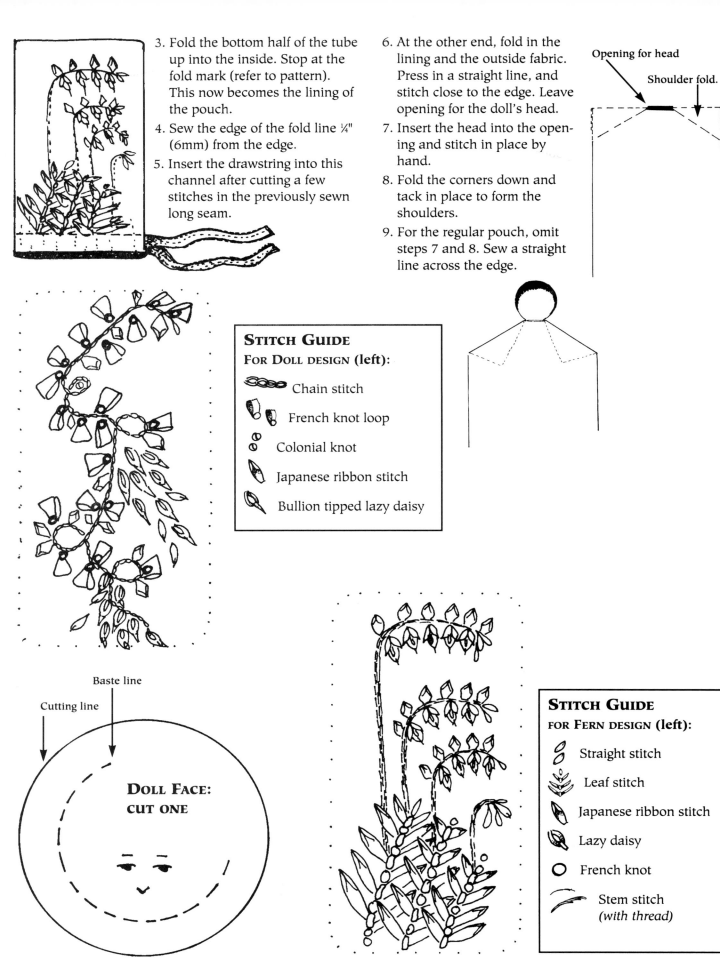

3. Fold the bottom half of the tube up into the inside. Stop at the fold mark (refer to pattern). This now becomes the lining of the pouch.

4. Sew the edge of the fold line ¼" (6mm) from the edge.

5. Insert the drawstring into this channel after cutting a few stitches in the previously sewn long seam.

6. At the other end, fold in the lining and the outside fabric. Press in a straight line, and stitch close to the edge. Leave opening for the doll's head.

7. Insert the head into the opening and stitch in place by hand.

8. Fold the corners down and tack in place to form the shoulders.

9. For the regular pouch, omit steps 7 and 8. Sew a straight line across the edge.

Opening for head

Shoulder fold.

STITCH GUIDE
FOR DOLL DESIGN (left):

Chain stitch

French knot loop

Colonial knot

Japanese ribbon stitch

Bullion tipped lazy daisy

STITCH GUIDE
FOR FERN DESIGN (left):

Straight stitch

Leaf stitch

Japanese ribbon stitch

Lazy daisy

French knot

Stem stitch *(with thread)*

Baste line

Cutting line

DOLL FACE:
CUT ONE

9. Embroidered Photographs

In my second book *Crazy Quilt Odyssey*, I talked about the Australian photocopy method. While experimenting with this technique, I discovered that acrylic paints could be diluted to watercolor consistency and painted over the photograph on fabric. Next, embroidery was added and I had found a new hobby! You will enjoy making these personal mementos. Use a fine silk to ensure a clearer copy. The embroidery patterns are made to fit 4" x 2½" (10cm x 6.3cm) ovals, 7" x 5" (18cm x 13cm) ovals, and 3" x 4½" (8cm x 10.3cm) rectangles.

MATERIALS:

Clear photograph, card, or magazine picture
10" (25cm) square of silk fabric or silk organza

Photocopy of photograph	Cotton balls
Natural gum turpentine	Ink blotting paper
Large metal spoon	Water erasable pen
6" (15cm) embroidery hoop	Tacky glue

Acrylic fabric paints: pink, turquoise, blue, green
(I use Ceramcoat™ by Delta)

⅓ yard (30cm) pellon fleece   Brush for paint

Picture mats and frames

DIRECTIONS:

1. Make a photocopy of the photograph or card–be sure it is crisp and clear. (It must be a black and white photocopy made with dry toner, not a laser or color copy print.) Obtain appropriate photocopy permission for copyrighted work.
2. Lay the fabric on top of the blotting paper.
3. Lay the photocopy face down on the fabric.
4. Soak the cotton ball in turpentine, squeeze out excess, and rub on the back of the photocopy. You will see the paper become translucent (as if oil had been spilled on it). Rub the area well–but don't get sloppy!
5. Rub the back of the spoon firmly across the photocopy. Rub evenly, holding the photocopy down with the other hand. When you are satisfied that you've rubbed the whole area, lift up a corner to check. If the image is not satisfactory, repeat the process.
6. Note that the image is reversed–hence organza works well because it is sheer. The image can be turned around to face correctly (especially useful with lettering!)
7. Dilute acrylic paint (colors of your choice) to a watercolor consistency. (I actually use watercolor paints myself). Paint lightly over the fabric photo. Allow the colors to blend into each other.
8. After your photo has been painted, choose the embroidery design and transfer it to the photo. Mark the actual outline on the photo with water erasable pen.
9. Move fabric to a hoop and work the embroidery stitches.

MEMORY BOUQUET DESIGN

Stitch Guide for Memory Bouquet is on page 85.

WHEAT & BRAMBLE BERRIES DESIGN

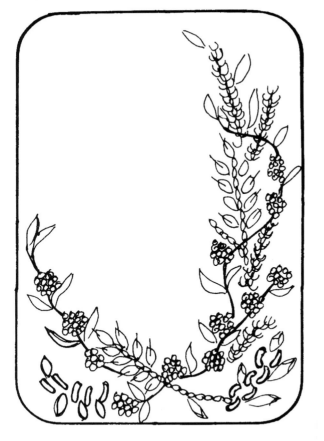

BEATRICE'S BOUQUET DESIGN

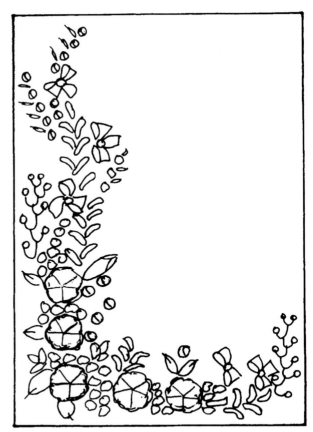

CATTAILS DESIGN

BABY BOUQUET DESIGN

Memory Bouquet

(Size: 4½" x 6½" or 8cm oval)

Silk thread or embroidery floss: two shades of green.

4mm silk ribbon: turquoise, lavender, pale pink, medium pink, peach, yellow, cream, gold, pale blue, medium blue, dusty pink, pale orange.

7mm ribbon: lavender silk ombre ribbon

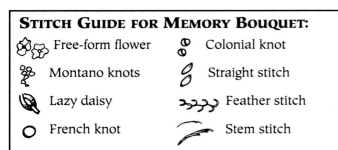

STITCH GUIDE FOR MEMORY BOUQUET:

Free-form flower		Colonial knot
Montano knots		Straight stitch
Lazy daisy		Feather stitch
French knot		Stem stitch

Wheat and Bramble Berries

(Size: 3½" x 5" or 9cm x 13cm rectangle)

Silk thread or embroidery floss: two shades of gold, light green, pale orange

4mm silk ribbon: gold, pale orange, three shades of red, rose red, three shades of green

STITCH GUIDE FOR WHEAT & BRAMBLE:

Straight stitch		Chain stitch
French knot		Japanese ribbon stitch
Feather stitch		Lazy daisy
Curved whip stitch		

Beatrice's Bouquet

(Size: 3½" x 5"or 9cm x 13cm rectangle)

Silk thread or embroidery floss: two shades of green.

4mm silk ribbon: dusty rose, light dusty rose, lavender, gold, cream, off-white, light teal, medium teal, pink, four shades of green.

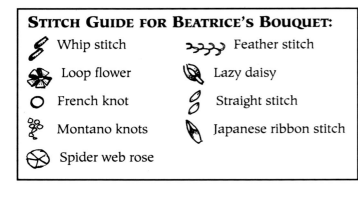

STITCH GUIDE FOR BEATRICE'S BOUQUET:

Whip stitch		Feather stitch
Loop flower		Lazy daisy
French knot		Straight stitch
Montano knots		Japanese ribbon stitch
Spider web rose		

Cattails (Size: 4" x 2½" or 10cm x 6.3cm oval)

Silk thread or embroidery floss: medium green and rust.

4mm ribbon: two shades of rust, teal, blue, dusty rose, medium orange, light blue and lavender, gold, three shades of green

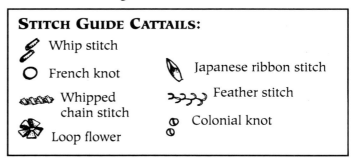

STITCH GUIDE CATTAILS:

Whip stitch		Japanese ribbon stitch
French knot		Feather stitch
Whipped chain stitch		Colonial knot
Loop flower		

Baby Bouquet

(Size: 4" x 2½" or 10cm x 6.3cm oval)

Silk thread or embroidery floss: pale rust

4mm silk ribbon: lavender, blue, dusty pink, medium teal, gold, cream, pale blue, pale pink, three shades of green, medium purple

STITCH GUIDE FOR BABY BOUQUET:

Spider web roses		Lazy daisy
Plume stitch		Japanese ribbon stitch
French knot		Whip stitch
Montano knots		Feather stitch

ASSEMBLY FOR EMBROIDERED PHOTOGRAPHS:

1. Lay the work face down into a thick terrycloth towel and press from the back. Be careful not to press too hard.
2. Mark the oval cutout with a water erasable pen on the finished piece.
3. Cut ½" (12mm) beyond the oval line.
4. Use a double mat.
5. Lay a bead of tacky glue on the inside of the first mat.
6. Glue the embroidered piece in place. Tape edges. Allow to dry thoroughly.
7. Cut out two ovals from the pellon fleece, exactly on the cutting line. Cut a third fleece ¼" (6mm) larger than the opening.
8. Lay the largest fleece on the back of the finished piece, then add the last two ovals.
9. Spread glue liberally on the art board backing. Lay the mat onto the backing and press firmly till dry (use books for weight).
10. Glue the second mat in place to complete the picture.

10. Garden Path

(Size: 5" x 7" or 13cm x 18cm)

 reate your own original ribbon-embroidered painting with these simple directions. The ribbon work adds a textured quality to the piece. Each little painting takes on its own personality.

MATERIALS:

12" (30cm) square of even-weave linen or cotton

⅓ yd. (30cm) pellon fleece   Water erasable pen

8" (20cm) embroidery hoop   Brushes

Permanent marking pens: Variety of embroidery
    sepia and black   yarns

Acrylic paints: green, purple, rose, blue, turquoise, sepia

Embroidery floss: two shades of green

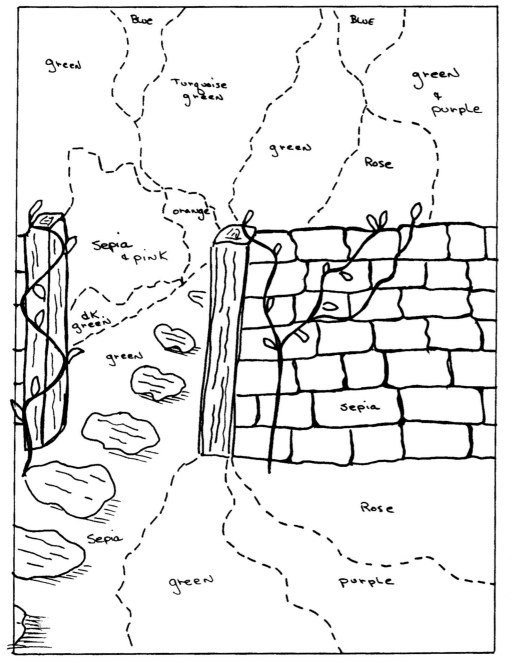

Broken lines – use water erasable pen for these lines

Solid lines – use permanent pens

4mm silk ribbon: light teal, medium teal, dark orange, medium orange, deep red, purple, dark purple, pale purple, gold, rose, cream, pale pink, pale lavender, pale peach, five shades of green

DIRECTIONS:

1. Mix up small amounts of paint. Dilute to a watercolor consistency.
2. Lay the fabric over the pattern, and with the water erasable pen, draw the tree areas and the foreground.
3. With the sepia permanent pen, draw the brick wall and gate posts. With the black permanent pen, draw the stepping stones.
4. Paint the sky area, the trees, and shrubs. Allow the paints to merge.
5. Paint the brick wall, the path, and foreground. Allow the paints to overlap like a watercolor.
6. Let the fabric dry completely. Iron to ensure permanence. Check for coloration and repeat some of the colors for a more pleasing effect if necessary.
7. Add more lines with the permanent pens.
8. Transfer the fabric to the embroidery hoop. Work the embroidery stitches in silk ribbon, floss, and yarn.

ASSEMBLY FOR GARDEN PATH:

1. Glue the finished piece into the first mat. Pull taut, tape edges, and let dry completely.
2. Follow directions for assembling picture as given on page 85.

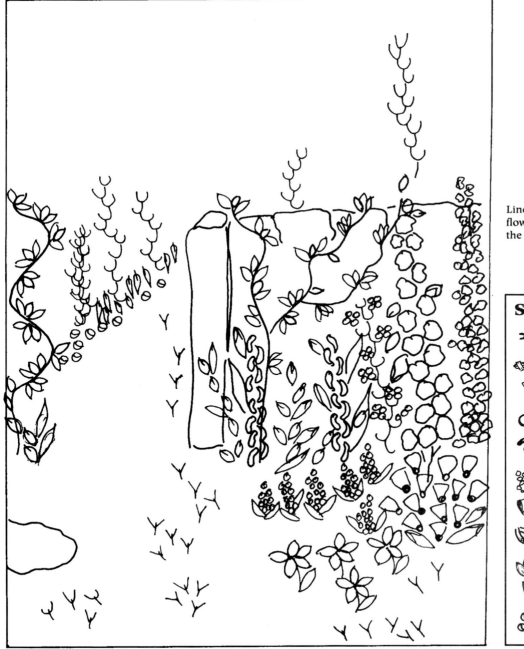

Line up rose bushes and draw in flowers with water erasable pen onto the painted fabric

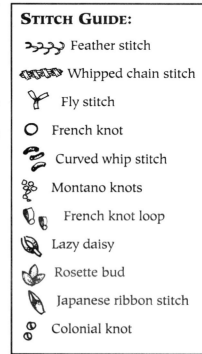

STITCH GUIDE:

Feather stitch

Whipped chain stitch

Fly stitch

French knot

Curved whip stitch

Montano knots

French knot loop

Lazy daisy

Rosette bud

Japanese ribbon stitch

Colonial knot

11. Floral Needle & Scissors Cases

(Size: 2½" x 4" or 6.3cm x 10cm)

he Victorian lady always displayed her sewing utensils in beautifully embroidered holders — all the better to subtly show off her needlework expertise. Here are two little beauties to protect and show off your favorite pair of embroidery scissors and prized needles. They look marvelous tied into a sewing basket.

MATERIALS (FOR BOTH PATTERNS):

20" (50cm) square of lightweight mat or poster board (has to be thinner than regular art board in order to bend and have enough "give" for the scissors holder)

20" (50cm) square of drapery-weight moiré

12" (30cm) square of iron-on interfacing

12" (30cm) length of ¼" (6mm) satin ribbon

6" (15cm) square felt for needle case

One 6" (15cm) length of double-sided satin

1½ yds. (137.4cm) length of rattail cord

Beads and #10 sharps beading needle

Nymo Thread and small metal snap

Chenille, tapestry, and embroidery needles

Tacky glue and spray adhesive craft glue

6" (15cm) embroidery hoop

Sheet of template plastic

4mm silk ribbon: dark pink, light pink, dusty pink, medium turquoise, gold, light turquoise, three shades of peach, four shades of green

Silk Buttonhole twist or embroidery floss: three shades of peach, four shades of green

Two 12" (30cm) lengths of ¼" (6mm) satin ribbon: peach and dusty pink

DIRECTIONS FOR SCISSORS HOLDER:

Score line → cut on opposite side of bend

1. Cut two backs and two fronts on the actual line of lightweight mat board or poster board. Set aside.

2. Trace with water-erasable pen the actual line of the scissors holder back and the embroidery design onto the moiré. Add the iron-on interfacing. Transfer this to a hoop and work the embroidery. Add beads to finish off.

3. Cut out the finished piece on the ½" (12mm) cutting line. Cut a second back in the same manner and set aside.

4. Cut two fronts on the cutting lines.

ASSEMBLY FOR SCISSORS HOLDER:

1. Score the two poster board backs on the fold line. With the scored line on the outside, spray the art board with spray adhesive, lay the finished moiré piece on top and smooth in place.

2. Cover the two fronts in the same manner.

3. After the front and back units have been glued together, whipstitch the front to the back. Use a strong thread.

4. Lay a bead of glue around the outer edge and lay the rattail cord in place. Form a button loop at the top as shown, by starting at the right side fold point.

5. Sew snap in place.

DIRECTIONS FOR NEEDLE CASE:

1. Make window templates, marking ½" (12mm) cutting line.

2. Cut two poster boards on actual line. Score on the fold line. Set aside.

3. With the water-erasable pen, mark the actual lines of the needle case on the moiré fabric. Trace the embroidery design. Iron the interfacing onto the back side. Place in embroidery hoop, drawing material taut.

4. Work the embroidery, add beads, remove from the hoop, and cut on the ½" (12mm) cutting line.

5. Cut a second moiré on the cutting line and one of felt on the actual line (use pinking shears for a pretty edge).

6. Cut the double-sided satin ribbon to 6¼" (15.9cm).

ASSEMBLY FOR NEEDLE CASE:

1. Score the two poster board backs on the fold line. With the scored side out, cover with the moiré fabric exactly as you did for the scissors holder.

2. Clip the ½" (12mm) edges (as seen in the frame directions). Lay a bead of glue on the back along the edges. Fold the clipped fabric to the back.

3. Repeat the above process for the lining piece. Make sure the scored edge faces inside (this makes a better crease).

4. Spread a generous amount of glue on the uncovered sides of the needle case. Glue these two pieces together, making sure the folds match evenly. Wedge the double-sided satin ribbon between these two pieces on indicated line.

5. Lay a fine bead of glue on the inside crease and lay the felt in place.

6. Press under a heavy book until glue has thoroughly dried.

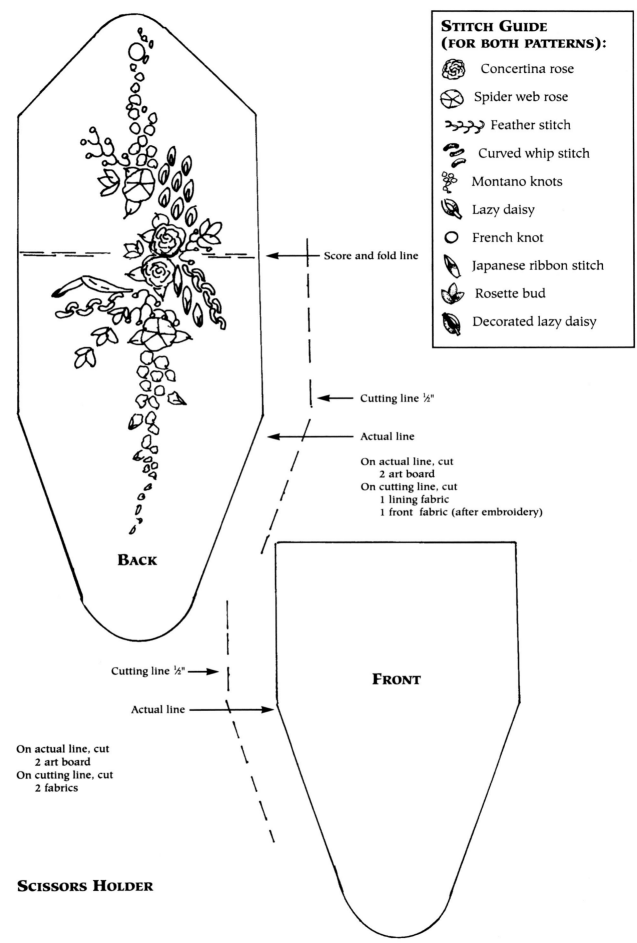

STITCH GUIDE
(FOR BOTH PATTERNS):

- Concertina rose
- Spider web rose
- Feather stitch
- Curved whip stitch
- Montano knots
- Lazy daisy
- French knot
- Japanese ribbon stitch
- Rosette bud
- Decorated lazy daisy

← Score and fold line

← Cutting line ½"

← Actual line

On actual line, cut
   2 art board
On cutting line, cut
   1 lining fabric
   1 front fabric (after embroidery)

BACK

Cutting line ½" →

Actual line →

On actual line, cut
   2 art board
On cutting line, cut
   2 fabrics

FRONT

SCISSORS HOLDER

NEEDLE CASE

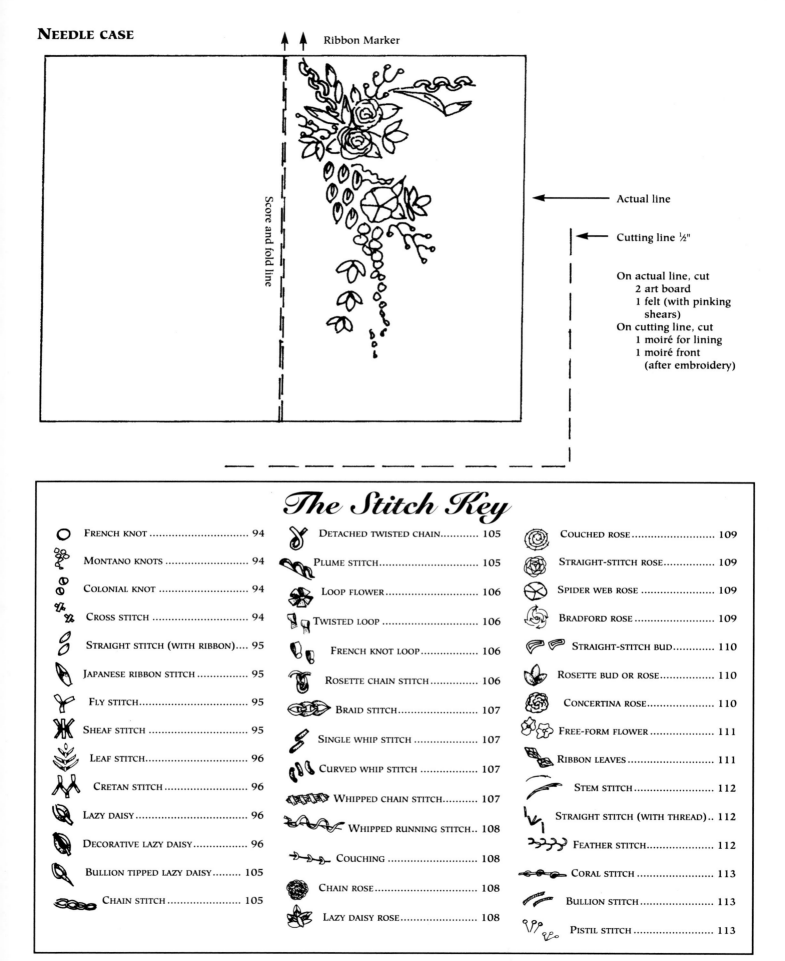

Ribbon Marker

Score and fold line

Actual line

Cutting line ½"

On actual line, cut
  2 art board
  1 felt (with pinking
    shears)
On cutting line, cut
  1 moiré for lining
  1 moiré front
    (after embroidery)

The Stitch Key

12. Wisteria Boudoir Set

isteria is a beautiful delicate blossom that appears in the spring for a far too brief period. I wanted to have wisteria around me all year long, and so created this boudoir set. The designs are reminiscent of the Edwardian era. While I have used Framecraft pieces, you can adapt these patterns to other projects and needlework containers.

MATERIALS:

Framecraft Miniatures Ltd. crystal jar — (Judith Designs - refer to Sources)

Framecraft brush and mirror set

⅓ yd. (30cm) black drapery-weight moiré

Chenille, tapestry, and embroidery needles

Beads, Nymo thread, #10 sharps beading needle

¼ yd. (24cm) pellon fleece

Tacky glue and spray adhesive

6" (15cm) embroidery hoop

Water erasable or white pen

½ yd. (48cm) each of five double-sided ¼" (6mm) satin ribbons: cream, lavender, dusty pink, dusty peach, dusty blue.

4mm ribbon: pale lavender, medium lavender, lavender blue, dusty pink, pale pink, cream, three shades of green

Silk buttonhole twist or embroidery thread: four shades of green, pale rust for trellis

DIRECTIONS FOR JAR:

1. Use the plastic insert as a pattern as this fits to the outside edge. Trace the actual line of the jar lid onto the moiré.

2. Transfer the embroidery design to the fabric and insert in an embroidery hoop.

3. Work the embroidery design. Add beads if you wish.

ASSEMBLY FOR JAR:

1. Cut the completed embroidered fabric on the actual line. (It is a bit scary, but it will fit exactly into the frame.)

2. Lay a bead of tacky glue along the inside lip of the jar lid. Lightly press fabric in place. Turn so the fabric rests upside down on the table. Allow to dry thoroughly.

3. Cut one pellon fleece on the actual line. Cut two that are ⅛" smaller. Stacking the largest one closest to the finished piece, add the other two and then insert the metal plate that holds it all in place. This allows the piece to have a nicely padded, much richer look.

WISTERIA DESIGN CRYSTAL BOWL LID

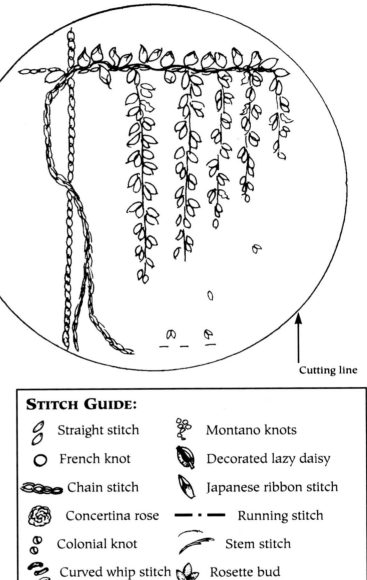

Cutting line

STITCH GUIDE:

Straight stitch	Montano knots
French knot	Decorated lazy daisy
Chain stitch	Japanese ribbon stitch
Concertina rose	— · — Running stitch
Colonial knot	Stem stitch
Curved whip stitch	Rosette bud

DIRECTIONS FOR BRUSH AND MIRROR:

The directions are exactly the same as for the jar lid.

ASSEMBLY FOR BRUSH AND MIRROR:

1. Disassemble the brush and mirror. The handle comes off and the outer metal rim of the brush and mirror can be loosened. Take out the metal plate behind the mirror and brush.

2. Cut one pellon fleece to fit on the back of this plate. Spread a thin layer of glue on the plate and set the pellon in place.

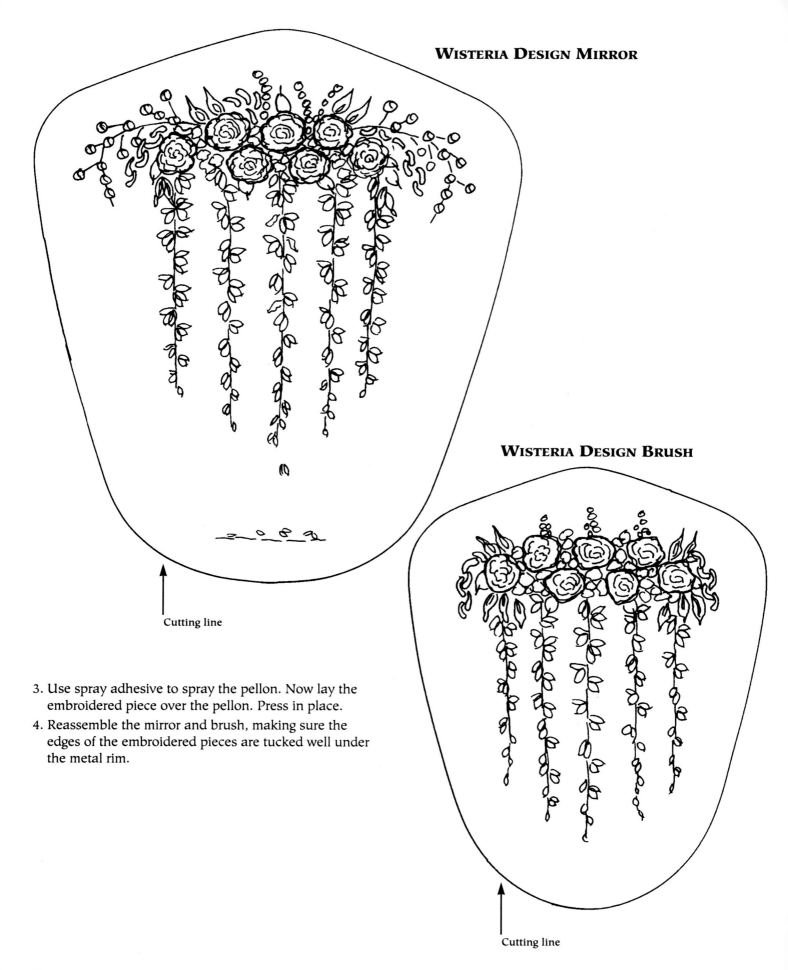

WISTERIA DESIGN MIRROR

WISTERIA DESIGN BRUSH

Cutting line

3. Use spray adhesive to spray the pellon. Now lay the embroidered piece over the pellon. Press in place.

4. Reassemble the mirror and brush, making sure the edges of the embroidered pieces are tucked well under the metal rim.

Cutting line

Silk Ribbon Stitch Guide

This stitch guide is designed for stitchers of all abilities. It is set up as a text and visual guide. First read the written directions, then follow through with the sketches. As you actually make the stitch, check the photographs for comparisons and flower examples. (Left handers can turn the page upside down.) The stitches are grouped into categories for your convenience. Be aware that the size of the stitch is affected by the width of the ribbon. (2mm ribbon small; 4mm ribbon, medium; 7mm ribbon, large). Most of the stitches can also be worked in thread.

Knots

FRENCH KNOT: Bring the needle up and circle the ribbon twice around the needle. Hold the ribbon off to one side as you insert the needle in the fabric as close to the starting point as possible. Hold the knot in place until the needle is pulled through. Examples: baby's breath, yarrow, etc.

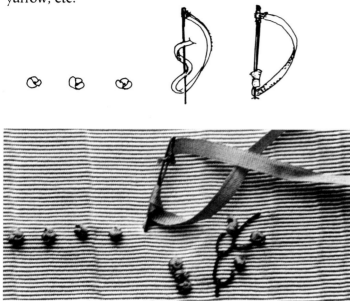

MONTANO KNOTS: Designed for the effect and not the technique! These glorified French knots are loose and effective for filling in and for floral sprays. Depending on the size desired, they vary from one to six twists.

Bring the needle up from the back and circle the ribbon around the needle (six, five, four, three, two, or one time). Hold the ribbon very loose and do not hold the ribbon off to one side. Insert the needle back into the fabric as close to the starting point as possible. Do not pull tight; let the knot remain loose and flowery.

COLONIAL KNOT: A lovely little knot that sits up and has a little dimple in the center. Come up from under the fabric at A. Form a backwards C with the ribbon. Insert the needle under the ribbon at the top of the backwards C.

Now grasp the ribbon and form a loop over and under the needle. This forms a figure 8 (B). Hold the needle vertically and pull the knot firmly around the needle. Insert the needle as close to the original hole (but not into it) as possible (C). Always hold the ribbon firmly in place until the needle is pulled to the back. This forms a neat colonial knot. Examples: rose buds, muscari, other tiny flower clusters.

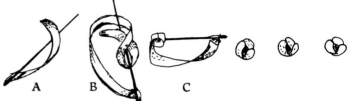

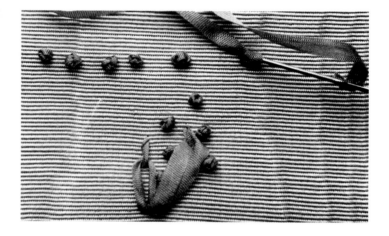

Straight Stitches

CROSS STITCH: These can be scattered or clustered for various floral effects. Bring the ribbon up at A. Go down at the top right corner at B. Keep the ribbon flat. Bring the ribbon back up at the top lefthand corner at C. Go back down at the lower right corner at D. (A small catch stitch either in ribbon or thread creates a small flower.)

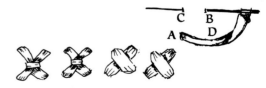

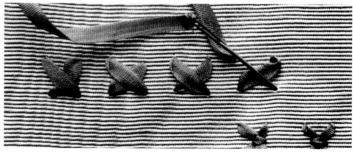

STRAIGHT STITCH (WITH RIBBON): This stitch may be taut or loose depending on the flower petal. Come up from under the fabric at A. Take the desired length and go down at B. Make sure the ribbon lies flat: Use your thumb to hold it flat or hold the ribbon in the loose hand and run the needle under the ribbon to its point A. Note: For a Running Stitch, continue in a straight line, keeping the ribbon flat. Examples: daisy petals, stems.

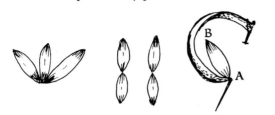

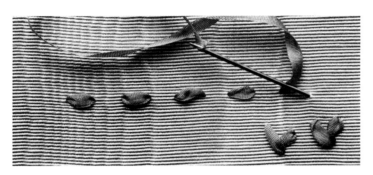

JAPANESE RIBBON STITCH: Come up from under the fabric at point A. Make sure the ribbon lies flat by running the needle under the ribbon. Lay the ribbon flat on the fabric and pierce the ribbon in the center at point B. Gently pull the needle through to the back. The ribbon will curl at the tip. (The whole effect will be lost if the ribbon is pulled too tightly.) Petals and leaves can be varied by length, and by adjusting the tension of the ribbon before piercing, it can be quite loose. Examples: blue bells, asters, lily, and iris leaves.

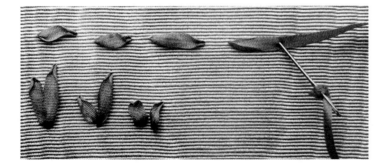

FLY STITCH: Come up at A and down at B. Hold the ribbon in a loop with the loose hand and bring the needle up at C, below and midway between A and B (forming a V). The needle passes over the ribbon. Draw through gently and anchor with a long or short catch stitch. Can be worked in a vertical row. Examples: iris-type flowers; vertically for cactus or stems.

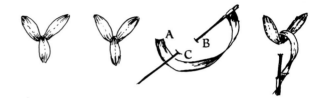

SHEAF STITCH: Three straight stitches are "tied" with a vertical stitch. Keep the tension loose. Come up at A and go down at B. Come up to the right at C and go down at D. Come up at E and go down at F. Now come up in the center midway between C and D and wrap at the center. Pull gently. The length of the straight stitches can be varied. The vertical stitch can be focused toward the top or the bottom. Examples: squill, lavender.

LEAF STITCH: This is a vertical stitch. Start with a vertical straight stitch A to B. Come up at C and make a loop. Pass the needle over the loop. Take a small catch stitch. Repeat the process, flaring out wider and wider. Example: ferns.

Flat Loop Stitches

LAZY DAISY: This stitch is a free-floating chain stitch. Bring the needle up from the back and hold the ribbon flat with your thumb (A). Insert the needle at the starting point so the ribbon forms a loop. Bring the needle out a short distance away. The needle passes over the ribbon. Take a small anchor stitch at the top of the loop. Length of the stitch and the anchor can be varied. Examples: petals and leaves.

CRETAN STITCH: This stitch starts in the bottom left corner and is worked left to right. Take short vertical stitches alternately downward and upward Hold the ribbon down so the needle will pass over it. The space between the vertical stitches can be altered. (This stitch can be worked evenly on each side of a seam.) Example: filler stitch.

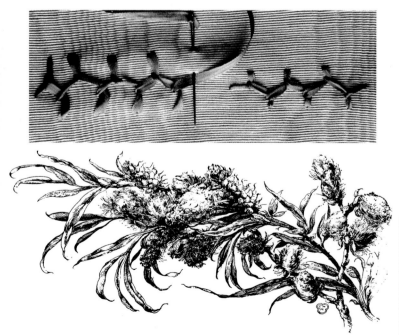

DECORATIVE LAZY DAISY: This is a simple lazy daisy with a straight stitch added. Come up at A and form a loop. Make sure the ribbon lies flat. Make a small catch stitch at B point. With another color, come up at A of the Lazy Daisy and go down inside of B. Examples: flower buds, sweet peas, lupines.

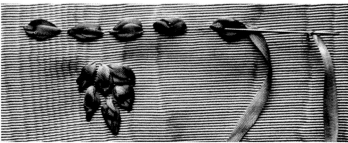

Above: Madeleine Montano wears the author's antique Haori, purchased at a Tokyo flea market for five dollars. Judith embellished the black collar area with silk ribbon work when flying (during take-offs and landings!) Hence the name "Take off and Landing Haori"! *(Photo: Bill O'Connor)*

Right: Detail of Haori. *(Photo: Alan Carter)*

Above left: Purchased garments can be further decorated with silk ribbon work. Judith purchased this art work rayon blouse and worked within the floral areas to create a soft feminine look. Ruth Madrid models while she enjoys reading in the author's sun room. *(Photo: Bill O'Connor)*

Right: Back view of rayon blouse — Ruth Madrid, model. *(Photo: Bill O'Connor)*

Left: When Jane Mueller purchased her dress for her daughter's wedding, the author added silk ribbon embroidery to the bodice and made a matching barrette. Sarah Smith models the barrette. Together they pose in Judith's backyard. *(Photo: Bill O'Connor)*

Above: Madeleine Montano wears her special crazy quilt vest made by her mother (Judith Montano). Her favorite colors, a tattered Chinese dragon pillow, African trade beads and silk ribbon embroidery are collaged together for a sophisticated piece worn over black silk shirt and pants. Madeleine poses in the family's perennial garden. *(Photo: Bill O'Connor)*

Right: Vest detail. *(Photo: Bill O'Connor)*

Above: Hat boxes are very popular in Australia. Judith decorated the lid of this one with elaborate crazy quilting, lace work, beading, doodads, ombre ribbon, and a spray of silk ribbon flowers *(Courtesy private collection of Gloria McKinnon. Photo: Alan Carter)*

Above right: Detail of floral spray on hat box. *(Photo: Alan Carter)*

Below: Silk ribbon embroidery jewelry spills across a rose-colored moiré box. All of these pieces, including the heart-shaped porcelain container, are by Framecraft Miniatures Limited of Great Britain. Judith has used silk ribbon, satin ribbon, and beads to create these exquisite works of art. (Framecraft pieces are available through Judith Designs — see source guide). *(Photo: Bill O'Connor)*

Above: Charming handkerchief pillow made from two antique hankies with silk ribbon and a white cotton pillow in the guest room have been given a second lease on life with a flower garden of silk ribbon embroidery. Judith has added all of her favorite flowers in a riot of colors. *(Photo: Bill O'Connor)*

Left: Detail of pillow. *(Photo: Bill O'Connor)*

Left: An elegant crazy quilt frame by the author is further highlighted with silk ribbon embroidery and flowers. Antique lace is shown off to great advantage. The matching clothes brush is adorned with silk and satin roses. *(Courtesy private collection of Gloria McKinnon. Photo: Alan Carter)*

Above: Detail of floral spray on frame. *(Photo: Alan Carter)*

Right: A study in peach, green, and cream. Alexandra Lober models her crazy quilt vest and belt made by the author. The vest is a collection of oriental and Australian fabrics. The antique and new laces are from England and France. The seams are embroidered with silk ribbons (knotted on the outside) and highlighted with fresh-water seed pearls. A spray of silk flowers provides a permanent corsage. *(Photo: Alan Carter)*

Below: Detail of floral spray, Alex's vest. *(Photo: Alan Carter)*

Below right: A purchased belt has been embellished by the author to pull together a Christmas outfit for Alexandra Lober. Buttons, silk and satin ribbons, and beads were sewn onto the figure-eight clasp. *(Photo: Alan Carter)*

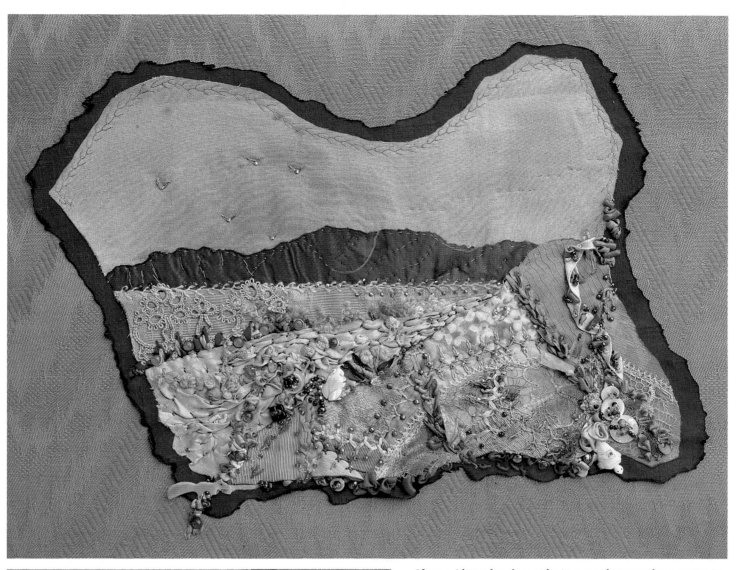

Above: After a few drops of rain a wondrous garden appears in the hills of New Mexico. *The Desert Garden* is a study in pale green, peach, and lavender, a mixed media of needlework techniques. Judith has used hand-dyed silks, antique fabrics, burned edges, crazy quilting, silk ribbon embroidery, crystals, beads, fetishes, and a mixture of threads and yarns. *(Photo: Bill O'Connor)*

Left: Detail of The Desert Garden. *(Photo: Bill O'Connor)*

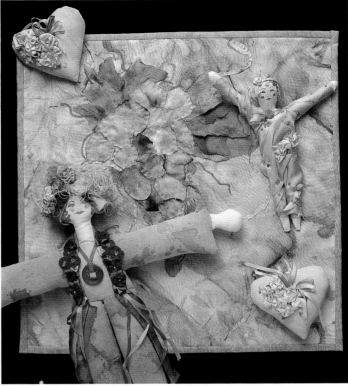

Above: Yvonne Porcella has been working with silk ribbon for many years. Her silk quilts and clothing are decorated with meandering silk ribbons. Yvonne started making dolls and hearts with her daughter, Suzanne Porcella Byrd, when Suzanne was living in married-student housing at the University of California, Berkeley, while she and her husband were at school. They sold the hearts and dolls to pay for Nick's (the first of six children!) tuition at a private school. The small silk piece is a sample of a controlled burn to make a realistic composition. *(Photo: Bill O'Connor)*

Below: Although silk ribbon and threads are produced in Japan, silk ribbon embroidery is not popular there. Judith finally found a sample provided by her student, Mrs. Etsuko Kamatsu of Shizuoka. This beautiful flower was made by her younger sister, Ms. Kyoko Takaoka. She learned ribbon embroidery (totsuka shishya) in the cultural school. This detail is from a gray silk drawstring bag, a gift from the maker to her sister. *(Photo: Bill O'Connor)*

Above: In Queensland, Australia, the West Australian Eucalypt (gum tree) produces a glorious hot pink blossom. In the back of Ruth Stonely's Patchwork Shop, Judith saw this magnificent tree and wanted to commemorate it. Using silk fabrics and threads from the shop, she came up with the "Gum Nut Bag." Raw silk and voile were burned for the leaves. Silk thread and moiré ribbon were made into tassel flowers. The worms are silk ribbon whip stitches! *(Photo: Judith Montano)*

BULLION TIPPED LAZY DAISY: A most effective variation of the simple lazy daisy — a bullion stitch replaces the anchor stitch. The petal or leaf is changed depending on the length of the lazy daisy and the bullion stitch. Keep the ribbon flat and taut. Come up from the bottom at A and make a loop. Go down again at A. Come up at B (like a basic lazy daisy). Grasp the ribbon in the loose hand and loop it under the point of the needle. Keep the ribbon flat. Wrap the ribbon around the needle two or three times. Hold the bullion twists in place with your thumb and pull the needle through. Hold the bullion knot firmly on the fabric and in line with the twists. Anchor the bullion knot by going down through the fabric. Examples: shooting stars, leaves.

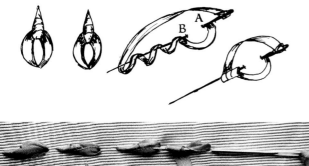

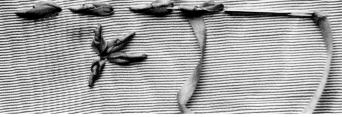

CHAIN STITCH: Starts the same as a lazy daisy except that it is continuous. Pull the ribbon up at the starting point A and hold it down with your thumb, forming a loop. Put the needle back down into point A and come up at B a short distance away. Bring the needle up over the ribbon, forming a small loop; repeat this stitch, making a chain. Examples: stems and vines (work in floss or 2mm ribbon).

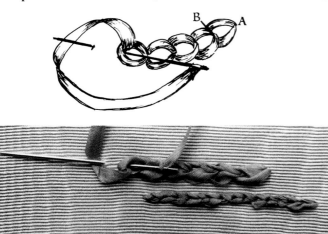

DETACHED TWISTED CHAIN: Come up at A and hold the ribbon flat with your thumb. Go down at B even with and to the left of A. Hold the ribbon in a loop and bring the needle up at C, below and midway between A and B. Anchor with a long or short catch stitch. Examples: buds and leaves.

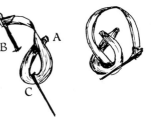

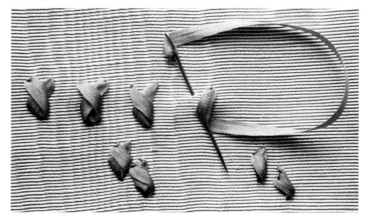

Dimensional Loop Stitches

PLUME STITCH: Worked from top to bottom. Come up at A and go down ⅛" away at B. Keep the ribbon flat at all times. Make a loop — control it with a round toothpick. Hold the loop in place with your thumb and come up at C piercing the fabric and ribbon. Form another loop. Continue down until the plume is finished. Examples: astilbe, ferns; good fillers.

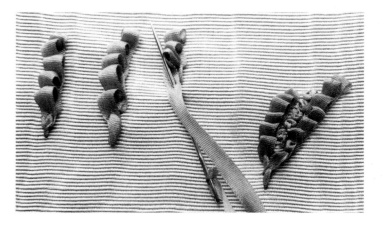

LOOP FLOWER: For the larger flowers, use 7mm ribbon and a large-eyed needle. Draw a small circle and mark the points of each petal (three, five, six) Come up in the circle at the center of the flower; go down ⅛" from this point. Adjust the loop over a round toothpick (a knitting needle or a large needle will work also). Keep the toothpick in the loop until you come up for the next loop to avoid pulling the last petal out of shape. After all the petals are worked, thread an embroidery needle with floss. Work the centers with French knots or pistil stitch to anchor the loops. Examples: pansies, briar rose (five petals); California poppy, evening primrose (four petals); thistledown (three petals).

TWISTED LOOP: This is a free-form stitch. Purposely twist the loop once and go down through the fabric. Good for plumes and frilly flowers like iris. Use the toothpick or needle to hold the loop until you've taken the next stitch down.

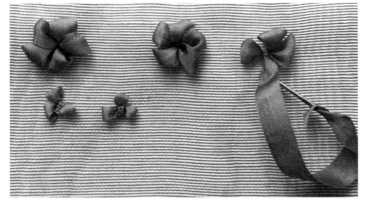

FRENCH KNOT LOOP: For this stitch you will need a straight pin to hold the loop in place while you make the French knot. Come up from the back of the fabric. Form a loop and hold it in place with the pin. Wrap the ribbon

twice around the needle. Insert the needle close to the pin and gently pull the knot into place. Hold the ribbon taut. Gently pull the needle through to the back. (use a colonial knot for variety).
Examples: single florettes or grouped for lupine-type flowers.

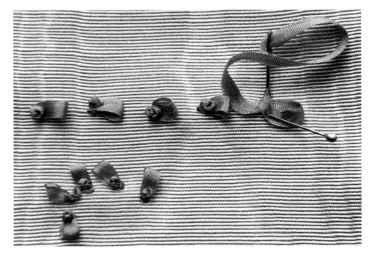

Braided Stitches

ROSETTE CHAIN STITCH: This stitch is worked from right to left. Use a blunt needle. Come up at A and go down at B a little to the left and below A. Come up at C slightly to the right and below B. Hold the ribbon across in front of the needle and keep it flat. Loop the ribbon under the needle. Pull through gently. Now slide the needle under the stitch at A. Pierce through the fabric to the back to complete a single stitch. Continue as shown to make a row. Space the rosettes far apart or closer, depending on the effect you want. Examples: heath, heather

BRAID STITCH: Use a blunt needle. Make a chain stitch with a small catch stitch. Go back down at C. Come up at D. Slide the needle behind the chain stitch and come back down at D. Come up at E. Slide the needle under the B-C anchor stitch as well as the previous chain stitch. Form another chain stitch and go down at E. Come up at F and go back two stitches. Slide the needle from right to left under both stitches. Continue this way sliding the needle from right to left under the two previous stitches together until the desired length is reached. Examples: grains, such as wheat, rye.

CURVED WHIP STITCH: Keep the ribbon flat. Make a straight stitch the desired length, A to B. Bring the needle up again at A. Wrap the straight stitch two or three times, working toward B and keeping the ribbon flat. Repeat the wraps working toward A. Anchor the last wrap stitch by passing the needle to the back. Crowd the stitch so it will curve. Examples: buds, roses, honeysuckle, broom.

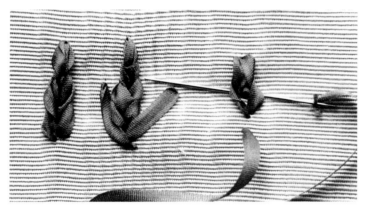

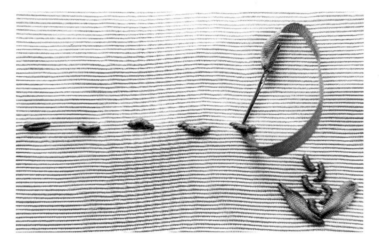

Whipped Stitches

SINGLE WHIP STITCH (Grub Stitch, Maggot Stitch, Sausage Stitch): Whatever the name, this is a very easy, effective stitch. Take a single straight stitch A to B. Bring the needle up again at A. Wrap the straight stitch two or three times depending on the effect desired. Keep the ribbon flat. Go down on the side to the back.
Examples: seeds, gladioli, buds.

WHIPPED CHAIN STITCH: Using a matching color of embroidery floss, make a row of continuous chain stitch. Use a blunt end needle and come up at the end. Roll the ribbon around each individual stitch. Keep the ribbon flat. Example: stems.

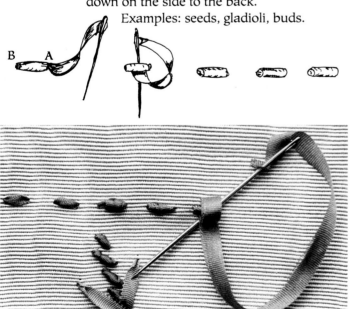

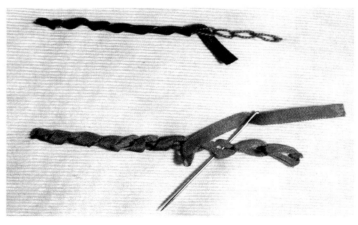

WHIPPED RUNNING STITCH: Using ribbon, make a line of running stitches. Make the stitches slightly wider than the width of the ribbon. The space between the stitches should be as close as possible. Change to a blunt-end needle for the whipped stitches. Go under the first running stitch keeping the ribbon flat. Make two whipped stitches per running stitch. Pull these two whipped stitches to make them wrap firmly. Move to the next stitch taking care not to pull as tight. Make two wrapped stitches and continue on. Remember to keep the ribbon flat. Examples: stems, fill-in for nuts and berries.

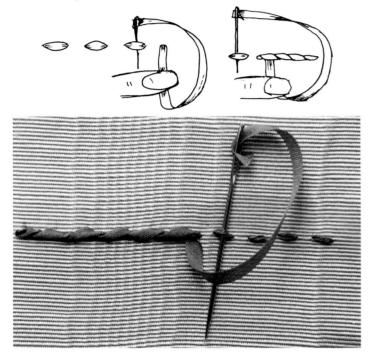

COUCHING: Lay the threads or ribbon flat on the fabric in the design you want. Now with either matching or contrasting thread or ribbon, come up from underneath and wrap a small, tight stitch over the flat thread or ribbon. Ribbon will take on a gathered look. Examples: stems, reeds.

Roses and Buds

CHAIN ROSE: This stitch is worked in a circle in a continuous chain stitch. Draw circle. Come up at the center and work the chain stitches in a tight spiral. Make one or two rows. Also good for chrysanthemums.

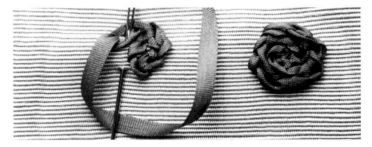

LAZY DAISY ROSE: Start at the top with a Japanese ribbon stitch A to B. Come up at the bottom of the leaf stitch at A and make a lazy daisy stitch. Angle it to the right of the ribbon stitch and go down at C. Come back down to the right of A at point D. Make a larger lazy daisy stitch angling to the left. Go down at E. Now thread with either a darker shade or green to make the base of the rose. Make a straight stitch angled to the right (this is tucked to the right of D). Lay a straight stitch along the outside of the left lazy daisy. The third stitch covers the base of the second straight stitch (along the right side of the left lazy daisy).

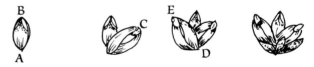

COUCHED ROSE: This stitch works best with 4mm or 7mm ribbon. It is a simple rose that is fast and effective. I use two needles threaded with a dark and light shade of ribbon. Start in the center with a U-shaped ribbon. Keep it loose and couch it once in the center. Now rotate around the center U couching the ribbon down. Keep the top ribbon loose.

SPIDER WEB ROSE: With perle cotton or embroidery floss, form the anchor stitch. Start with a fly stitch. Add a bar (of the same length) on each side forming five spokes. With the ribbon, come up in the center of the anchor spokes and begin weaving over and under the spokes. Allow the ribbon to twist and keep it loose. Fill in until the spokes are covered.

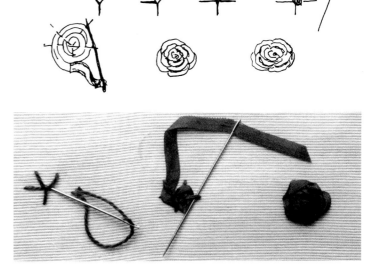

STRAIGHT-STITCH ROSE: Start in the center with a straight stitch angled to the right. Overlay the second straight stitch to cover the top of stitch 1. Now cover the base of stitch 2 with the third straight stitch and angle this one to the left. Now circle the center piece with seven straight stitches. Circle around in a second row, overlapping the previous row and overlapping the joining points of the first row with the longer straight stitch of the second row.

BRADFORD ROSE: Work a French knot or colonial knot for the center. Work three curved whipped stitches around the knot. Work in a clockwise direction. Anchor each stitch in a curve. Work four to five more curved whip stitches around the previous row. Always start the whipped stitch in the center of the previous stitch. Change the shade of the ribbon from dark to light.

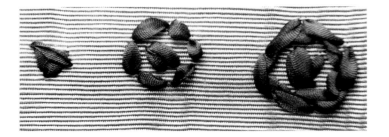

STRAIGHT-STITCH BUD: Make a padded straight stitch. Do not pull tight, and keep the ribbon flat. With embroidery floss, anchor the bud with a pistil stitch. With floss or 2mm ribbon, form the leaves and stem with a fly stitch.

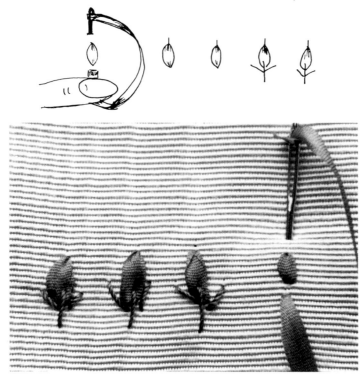

ROSETTE BUD OR ROSE: Make a padded straight stitch. Come up from the bottom at A. Insert needle at B making a small straight stitch. Come up at C and down at D creating a second straight stitch. Keep the ribbon flat.

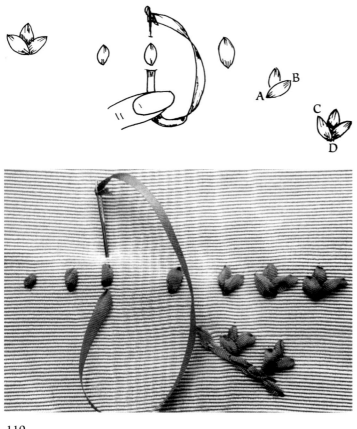

Satin Ribbon Work

hese flowers are worked in polyester and satin ribbon and set up higher on the fabric. Remember, the wider the ribbon, the larger the flower.

CONCERTINA ROSE: Use thread that matches ribbon, and thread needle, knotting the end. Use ⅛" (3mm) or ¼" (6mm) ribbon for the flowers. Cut a length of 10" (26cm). (For wider ribbon, cut a longer length.) Fold the ribbon at a right angle in the center (A). Fold the ribbon to the left (B). Bring the ribbon up on the bottom and fold it up and over (C). The folds will take on a square look (D). Keep folding from right side to top to left side to bottom until the ribbon is used up (about 20 times). Grasp the two ends in one hand and let go of the folded ribbon. It will spring up in accordion folds. Hold the two ends in one hand and pull gently down on one ribbon — it doesn't matter which one — until a rose is formed. With the knotted thread, go down through the top and up again (do this two or three times). Finish on the bottom and wrap the base tightly, make a slip knot, and cut the thread, leaving a 6" tail (to sew down later). Cut the two ends of the ribbon as close to the base as possible.

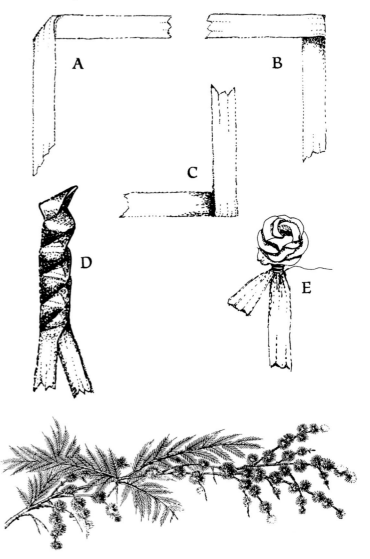

RIBBON LEAVES: Can be made from ribbon ⅛" to 2" wide (up to 5cm), depending on the size of the ribbon. Cut a ½" (12mm) ribbon, 1½" long (4cm). Fold it into a prairie point (with raw edges folded down to base). Baste along the wide edge. Pull the thread to gather. Make a knot and leave a tail for tacking. Tack the leaf down first and then the flower.

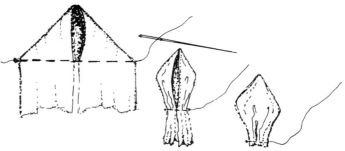

FREE-FORM FLOWERS: No two flowers are the same in a garden. Relax and have fun with these free-form ruffly flowers! For tiny flowers use narrow ribbon ⅛" to ¼" wide (2mm to 4mm) cut in 3" (8cm) lengths. For ½" to 1" ribbon (up to 2.5cm) cut 4" (10cm) lengths. Fold both ends and baste along one long edge. Gather tightly and knot. Whipstitch the folded ends together. Leave a tail for sewing on later.

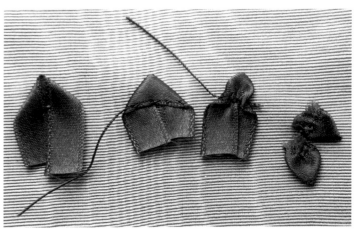

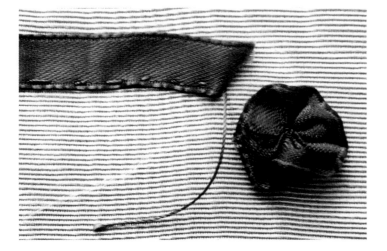

Embroidery Stitches

 se embroidery floss or silk buttonhole twist. These embroidery stitches are used as stems, branches and fillers. Many of the previous ribbon embroidery stitches can be worked in thread.

STEM STITCH: This stitch is worked from left to right. Sew along the designated line and keep the thread to the left of the needle. Come up in the center and on the right side of the previous stitch. Can be laid on in rows, side by side, as a covering stitch.

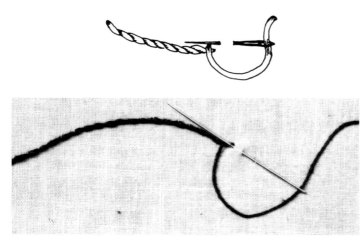

STRAIGHT STITCH (WITH THREAD): This is a wonderful fill-in stitch. Straight stitches can be worked evenly or irregularly. They can be long, short, or overlapping; in vertical, horizontal, or angled lines. Do not make the stitches too loose or too long because they can snag.

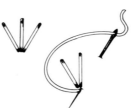

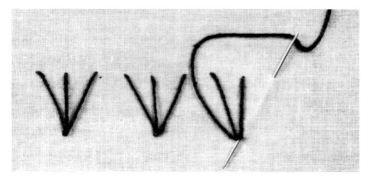

FEATHER STITCH (BRIAR STITCH, TURKEY TRACKS): This is a vertical stitch and alternates from right to left. It is worked from top to bottom. Begin with a single stitch. Come up at A and down at B; come up in the center below A and B at C. The secret is to always put the needle in at B straight across from where the thread came out at A.

CORAL STITCH: Work horizontally from right to left. While making a small stitch, hold the thread under the needle and draw the needle through to gently form the knot. The length of the vertical angled stitch determines the size of the knot. This can be worked successfully in ribbon.

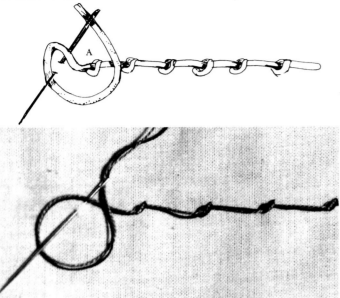

BULLION STITCH: Can be used in clusters, individually or side by side. Use double thread or silk buttonhole twist. Come up at A and go down at B, forming a small loop (a). Come up again at A and pull the thread halfway up through the material. Hold the needle from below and twist the thread around the needle until the twists equal the distance between A and B (c). Hold the top of the needle with the thumb and finger of the loose hand and draw the needle through the twists (d). Use the needle to hold the twists while pulling the thread through until the knot lies flat on the fabric (e). Put in the needle at the end of the twist and pull through firmly.

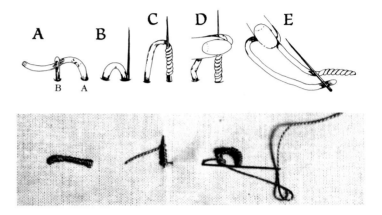

PISTIL STITCH. Use this stitch for flower centers or for free-form grass. Come up at A and form a French knot at the end of a short length of ribbon or thread. Go down at B (the length away from A of the thread plus French knot) and pull firmly into place.

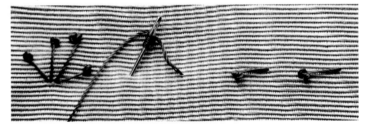

Source Guide

Magazines for Embroidery & Needle Arts:

The following magazines are varied and offer lists of exhibitions, workshops and up-to-date information, supplies and needlework supplies.

AUSTRALIA

❖ *Textile - Fiber Forum* [Published three times per year.]
A.F.T.A. Sturt Crafts Center
P.O. Box 192, Mittagong, N.S.W.
2575 Australia

❖ *Hand Made* [Quarterly]
G.P.O. Box 5252, Sydney, N.S.W.
2001 Australia

ENGLAND:

❖ *Crafts* [Six times per year]
The Craft Council,
8 Waterloo Place
London SW1 4AT England

❖ *Embroidery*
The Embroiderer's Guild
Apt. 41, Hampton Court Palace
East Molessy
Surrey KT8 9AU England

UNITED STATES

❖ *Fiber Arts* [Six times per year]
Nine Press, 50 College Street,
Asheville, NC 28801 U.S.A.

❖ *The Flying Needle* [Quarterly]
National Standards Council of
American Embroiderers
3165 S. W. Ridgewood Drive
Portland, OR 97225 U.S.A.

❖ *Needle Art* [Quarterly]
The Embroiderers Guild of America
200 Fourth Ave.
Louisville, KY 40202 U.S.A.

❖ *Sew Beautiful* [Quarterly]
518 Madison Street
Huntsville, AL 35801 U.S.A.

❖ *Threads* [Six times per year]
Taunton Press Inc.
P.O. Box 5506
Newtown, CT 06470 U.S.A.

Profile Personalities:

These needlework experts would appreciate hearing from you whether for workshop information or just to exchange ideas.

E. LYNNE BOWDEN

"Briarhurst"
19 Kelly Place
Chartwell, Hamilton
New Zealand

Willing to teach throughout New Zealand and internationally if time can be arranged.

JENNY BRADFORD

P.O. Box 5
Scullin, A.C.T.
2614 Australia
Fax: 61-6-2546814

Classes vary from one to four days. Will teach locally, nationally, and internationally.

PUBLICATIONS:

❖ *Simply Smocking and Simply Smocking 2*
(published in U.S.A. as one volume)
Sterling Publishing Co.
387 Park Avenue South
New York, NY 10016 U.S.A.

❖ *Silk Ribbon Embroidery for Gifts and Garments, Bullion Stitch Embroidery for Roses to Wildflowers, Original Designs for Silk Ribbon Embroidery*
Sally Milner Publishing Pty. Ltd.
67 Glassop St.
Birchgrove, N.S.W.
2041 Australia

❖ *Silk Ribbon Embroidery — Australian Wildflower Designs,*
Silk Ribbon Embroidery 2 — Transform Your Clothes
Greenhouse — Penguin Books
Australia
487 Maroondah Highway —
P.O. Box 247
Ring Wood, Victoria
3134 Australia

DENISE BRICE

#8 Helen Court
Cheltenham, Victoria
3192 Australia

Workshops in wool and silk ribbon embroidery. Locally, nationally, and internationally

WILANNA BRISTOW

344 Wildrose Avenue
San Antonio, TX 78209 U.S.A.

Willing to teach local, national, or international classes.

PUBLICATIONS:

❖ *Patterns with Potential*
Wilanna Bristow & Cecilia Steinfeldt,
San Antonio Museum Association,
San Antonio, TX, 1984.

❖ *The Sublime Heritage of Martha Mood,*
Vol II The Final Chapter
Kierstead Publications
Monterey, CA, 1983.

❖ *Fundamentals of Color*
Wilanna Bristow and Bill Bristow
Self-published
Correspondence Course for the
Embroiderers Guild of America, 1978.

JEAN FOX

501 S. Fannin
San Benito, TX 78586 U.S.A.

Will teach locally and nationally and will consider international workshops.

REMONA GIBESON

6425 E. 55th Terrace
Kansas City, MO 64129-2554
U.S.A.

Will teach doll and embroidery classes; locally, nationally and internationally.

PUBLICATIONS:

❖ *Victorian Ribbon Embroidery for Dolls*
by Remona Gibeson
Maureen Gueeson, Publisher
510 Ellington Road
South Windsor, CT 06074 U.S.A.

HEATHER JOYNES
98 Mill Street
Carlton, N.S.W.
2218 Australia

Two-day seminars for beginners and advanced. Teaches locally, nationally, and internationally.

PUBLICATIONS:
❖ *Ribbon Embroidery — Creative Ribbon Embroidery and Stitches for Embroidery*
David Rosenberg
Kangaroo Press
3 White Hall Road
Kenthurst N.S.W.
2156 Australia

GLORIA MCKINNON
c/o Anne's Glory Box
60 Beaumont Street
Hamilton, N.S.W.
2303 Australia
Fax: 61-049-616587

Will teach locally, nationally, and internationally; one-day to two-day workshops, project oriented.

KAYE PYKE
359 Bay Street
Port Melbourne, Victoria
3207 Australia

Teaches locally, nationally, and internationally; one-day to two-day workshops, project oriented.

PUBLICATIONS:
❖ *Kaye Pyke's Elegant Embroidery*
by Kaye Pyke and Lynne Landy
Kaye Pyke's Classic Cushions
Allen & Unwin Pty. Ltd.
292 Rathdowne Street
Carlton North, Victoria
3054 Australia

MERRILYN HEAZELWOOD
P.O. Box 615
Sandy Bay, Tasmania
7005 Australia
Teaches locally, nationally, and internationally; one-day and two-day workshops, project oriented.

PUBLICATIONS:
❖ *Spring Bulb Sampler, Fuchsias,* and *Roses.*

ELIZABETH MOIR
1 Edwards Green
Floreat Park, W.A.
6014 Australia

Teaches locally, nationally and internationally. Specializes in one day workshops and seminars of two days or more.

JUDITH MONTANO
P.O. Box 177
Castle Rock, Colorado 80104 U.S.A.

Teaches locally, nationally, and internationally. Mixed media of classes.

PUBLICATIONS:
❖ *Crazy Quilt Handbook, Crazy Quilt Odyssey: Adventures in Victorian Needlework,* and *Recollections*
C & T Publishing
P.O. Box 1456
Lafayette, CA 94549 U.S.A.

Sources: Retail & Wholesale

SASE: Self-addressed, Stamped Envelope (*When sending a request to a foreign country, send the equivalent of $1 U.S. for postage.*)
S.I.: Ships International

AUSTRALIA
Anne's Glory Box
60-62 Beaumont Street
Hamilton, N.S.W.
2303 Australia

Complete line of needlework supplies, laces, and books. Retail and wholesale SASE (business size #10 envelope) S.I.

Cotton on Creations
P.O. Box 556
Mittagong, N.S.W.
2575 Australia

Silk ribbons, threads, quality laces, fine fabrics, books. SASE; S.I.

Mary Hart-Davies
P.O. Box 6
Somers, Victoria
3927 Australia

Beautiful hand-dyed silk ribbon, wool, fabric, and threads. SASE; S.I.

The Raw Material
15 Lakeview Drive
Wallaga Lake, N.S.W.
Australia

Range of silk and cotton fabrics suitable for dyeing and hand printing. SASE for samples and prices S.I.

Ruth's Patchwork Supplies
43 Gloucester Street
High Gate Hill
Brisbane, Queensland
4101 Australia

Fine fabrics, needlework supplies and unusual threads and ribbons. Quarterly Newsletter. For mail order, send SASE; S.I.

CANADA:
Cloth Shop
4515 West 105th Avenue
Vancouver, British Columbia
V6R 2H8 Canada

32-page catalog $3.00 S.I.

Silver Thimble Inc.
64 Rebecca Dept. cq.
Oakville, Ontario
L6K 1J2 Canada

E L F Design Studio
5014 51st Street
Olds, Alberta
TOM IPO Canada

Incredible selection of fabrics and crazy quilt supplies. Catalog $2.50 S.I.

UNITED STATES

❊ ❊ ❊ GENERAL ❊ ❊ ❊

Aardvark Adventures in Handcrafts
P.O. Box 2449, Dept. cq
Livermore, CA 94550 U.S.A.

Stamps, buttons, a wide variety of threads and supplies. Publishes a marvelous newspaper/catalog. Send two first-class U.S. stamps and return address.

Very Victorian Notions
(formerly Judith Designs)
P.O. Box 18-M
Denver, CO 80218 U.S.A.

Featuring the most complete assortment of ribbon embroidery items and supplies. Send $3.00 US or $5.00 international post reply coupons for catalog.

Bernina of America, Inc.
534 W. Chestnut
Hindsdale, IL 60521 U.S.A.

Judith uses a Bernina sewing machine exclusively and loves it! Please write for more information.

YLI Corporation
Provo, Utah

BEADS, BUTTONS, ETC.

Eagle Feather Trading Post
168 West 12th Street
Ogden, UT 84404 U.S.A.

Beadwork supplies. Catalog, $3.

Shipwreck Beads
5021 Mud Bay Road
Olympia, WA 98502 U.S.A.

Over 2,000 beads! Color catalog, $3.

Small Wonders
1317 S.E. Boulevard
Spokane, WA 99202 U.S.A.

Sterling and 14K gold charms and thimble cages. Send SASE. S.I.

✳ ✳ ✳ EMBROIDERY ✳ ✳ ✳

Things Japanese
9805 N.E. 116th Street, Suite 7160
Kirkland, WA 98034 U.S.A.

Japanese silk filament, ribbon, thread. Catalog and swatches, $4. S.I.

✳ ✳ FABRICS & DYES ✳ ✳

Cerulean Blue
P.O. Box 21168
Seattle, WA 92888-3168 U.S.A.

All types of supplies for the dyer and painter of fabric. Color catalog, $4.50.

Island Fibers
RT Box 104
Washington Island, WI 54246 U.S.A.

A complete line of silk ribbon, dyed fabrics, threads, and yarns. Variegates are a specialty. Send SASE + $2.00*

Shades
2880 Holcomb Br. Road
Box 9, Dept. cq
Alpharetta, GA 30201 U.S.A.

Dyed cottons and silks by the yard. Catalog, $5.

Thai Silks
252 State Street, Dept. cq
Los Altos, CA 94022 U.S.A.

The largest selection of silk materials — very reasonable. Send SASE for catalog information. S.I.

Yvonne Porcella Studios
3619 Shoemake Avenue
Modesto, California 95351 U.S.A.

Books and patterns. Dyed fabrics by order only. Commissions accepted. Send SASE for catalog. S.I.

✳ ✳ FRAMES & BOXES ✳ ✳

Tennessee Wood Crafters
P.O. Box 239
Springfield, TN 37172 U.S.A.

Wood boxes, frames, decorative wood items for needlework insertion. Send SASE for catalog. S.I.

✳ ✳ ✳ LACE ✳ ✳ ✳

Heirlooms by Emily
R.D. #1, Box 190
Glen Rock, PA 17327 U.S.A.

Laces, Swiss batiste, inserts, borders. Catalog, $2.50.

✳ ✳ PUNCH NEEDLE ✳ ✳

Bernadine's Igolochkoy™
411 Crestwood Drive
Arthur, IL 61911 U.S.A.

Punch needles, supplies, patterns, kits, threads, yarns. Catalog, $2 (refundable with first order). S.I.

Birdhouse Enterprises
110 Jennings Ave. Dept JM
Patchogue, NY 11772

Punch needles in three sizes, gauges, special hoops, and instruction books. Send SASE and $1.00 for catalog S.I.

✳ TOOLS & SUPPLIES ✳

Anne Powell Ltd.
P.O. Box 3060
Stuart, Florida 34995 U.S.A.

Fine needlework tools and supplies, antique tools, books. Catalog, $5.

Clotilde Inc.
1909 S.W. 1st Avenue
Fort Lauderdale, FL 33315-2100
U.S.A.

Every type of sewing aid imaginable. Catalog, $2.

Lacis
2982 Adeline Street, Dept. JM
Berkeley, CA 99703 U.S.A.

Lacemaking tools, antique lace and materials, heirloom sewing supplies, books, needlework tools. Catalog, $4.

Martha Pullen Company, Inc.
518 Madison Street
Huntsville, AL 35801 U.S.A.

Heirloom sewing supplies, patterns, and books. S.I.

Quilter's Resources
2211 N. Elston
P.O. Box 148850
Chicago, IL 60614 U.S.A.

Silk ribbon, threads, trims, and sewing supplies. Free catalog. Wholesale only. S.I.

Darice Craft Supplies
P.O. Box 360284
Strongsville, OH 44136-6699 U.S.A.

Makers of music boxes. Wholesale only. Look in the phone book for retailers in your local area.

Elsie's Exquisiques
208 State Street
St. Joseph, MI 49085 U.S.A.
Call toll free: 1-800-742-SILK

Wholesale and retail source for ribbon, embroidery tools and materials. Catalog $2.50 S.I.

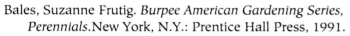

Bibliography

Bales, Suzanne Frutig. *Burpee American Gardening Series, Perennials.*New York, N.Y.: Prentice Hall Press, 1991.

Barton, Julia. *The Art of Embroidery.* London, England: Merehurst Press, 1989.

Beany, Jan. *The Art of The Needle.* London, England: Century Hutchinson Ltd., 1988.

_____. *Stitches: New Approaches.* London, England: BT. Batsford Limited, 1988.

Beaton, *Mrs. Beaton's Book of Needlework Consisting of Descriptions and Instructions.* London, England: Word, Lock and Co., n.d. (c. 1800s).

Bird, Richard. *Companion Planting.* London, England: Quarto Publishing Plc., 1990.

Body Blue Prints. *The Art and Craft of Ribbon Work.* Greenbrae, California: Body Blue Prints, 1989.

Bradford, Jenny. *Silk Ribbon Embroidery — Australian Wildflower Designs.* Ellwood, Victoria, Australia: Greenhouse Publications, 1988.

_____. *Silk Ribbon Embroidery II — Transform Your Clothes.* Ellwood, Victoria, Australia: Greenhouse Publications, 1989.

_____. *Silk Ribbon Embroidery III — For Gifts and Garments.* Birchgrove, N.S.W., Australia: Sally Milner Publishing Pty. Ltd., 1990.

Brainerd & Armstrong. *Silk Embroidery and Popular Fancy Work.* New London, Connecticut: 1898.

Briggs, Ruth. *Quilting and Related Needlework, Vol. 2, No. 1.* Rancho Santa Fe, California: Ruth Briggs Quilts, n.d.

Buczaki, Stefan: *Creating a Victorian Flower Garden.* London England: William Collins Sons and Co., Ltd., 1988.

Caulfield, S.F.A. *Encyclopedia of Victorian Needlework, Vol. I (A-L).* New York, N.Y.: Dover Publications, 1972.

Clayton-Payne, Andrew. *Victorian Flower Gardens.* London, England: Weidenfeld and Nicolson, Ltd., 1988.

Coats & Clark. *100 Embroidery Stitches.* New York, N.Y.: Ballantine Books, 1981.

Darling Kindersley Ltd. *The Pattern Library: Embroidery.* New York, N.Y.: Ballantine Books, 1981.

Decorative Stitches & Trimmings. London, England: Women's Institute of Domestic Science, 1928.

Dillmart, Therese. *Encyclopedia of Needlework.* Alsace, France: D.M.C. Library Mulhouse, 1800. [Reprint: Running Press, Pennsylvania, 1972.]

Druesdow, Jean L. In Style, *Celebrating Fifty Years of the Costume Institute.* New York, N.Y.: Metropolitan Museum of Art, 1987.

Frost, Annie. *Ladies' Guide to Needlework.* 1877.

Georgina, Kerr, Kaye. *Milinery for Every Woman.* England: 1926.

Gibbs, May. *Snuggle Pot and Cuddle Pie.* North Ryde, N.S.W., Australia: Collins/Angus and Robertson Publishers, 1990.

Hobhouse, Penelope and Wood, Christopher. *Painted Gardens, English Water Colours, 1850 - 1914.* New York, N.Y.: Athenium Macmillan Publishing Co., 1988.

Hodges, Felice. *Period Pastimes: A Practical Guide to Four Centuries of Decorative Crafts.* New York, N.Y.: Weidenfeld & Nicolson, 1989.

Holden, Edith. *The Country Diary of an Edwardian Lady.* Exeter, Devon, England: Michael Joseph, Webb and Bower Ltd., 1977.

Isaacs, Jennifer. *The Gentle Arts: 200 Years of Australian Women's Domestic and Decorative Arts.* Willoughby, Australia: Ure Smith Press, 1987.

Joynes, Heather. *Ribbon Embroidery.* Kenthurst, Australia: Kangaroo Press, 1988.

_____. *Creative Embroidery*. Kenthurst, Australia: Kangaroo Press, 1989.

Keladis, Gwen. *Penstemons For the Garden, Fine Gardening #20*. Newton, Connecticut: The Fountain Press Inc., 1991.

Marsh, Janet. *Nature Diary*. London, England: Michelin House, Peerage Books, 1984.

McLean, Mary Anne. *Mary Anne's Garden*. New York, N.Y.: Harry N. Abrams, Inc., n.d.

Metropolitan Art Series. *Needlecraft: Artistic and Practical*. New York, N.Y.: The Butterick Publishing Company, Ltd., 1890.

Montano, Judith A. *The Crazy Quilt Handbook*. Lafayette, California: C & T Publishing, 1988.

_____. *Crazy Quilt Odyssey, Adventures In Victorian Needlework*. Lafayette, California: C & T Publishing, 1991.

Morris, Barbara J. *The History of English Embroidery*. Bristol, England: Her Majesty's Stationery Office, 1951.

Morrison, Winefrede. *Ribbon Work*. n.d.

Nichols, Marion. *Encyclopedia of Embroidery Stitches, Including Crewel*. New York, N.Y.: Dover Publications, 1974.

Original Designs For Silk Ribbon Embroidery. Birchgrove, Australia: Sally Milner Publishing Pty. Ltd., 1991.

Ortho Book Editorial Staff. *The Easiest Flowers to Grow*. San Ramon, California: Ortho Books, 1990.

Parker, Freda. *Victorian Embroidery*. New York, N.Y.: Crescent Books, 1990

Peterson, Roger Tory, and Terenbaum, Frances. *A Field Guide to Wild Flowers Coloring Book*. Boston, Massachusetts: Houghton Mifflin Company, 1982.

Pyke, Kaye, and Landy, Lynn. *Elegant Embroidery*. Carlton North, Australia: Allen and Unwin Pty. Ltd., 1990.

_____. *Kaye Pyke's Classic Cushions*. Carlton North, Australia: Allen and Unwin Pty. Ltd., 1991.

Sinnes, A. Cort. *All About Perennials*. San Francisco, California: Ortho Books, 1981.

Sorkin, Gerri. *Keepsake Transfer Collection: Just Flowers*. Berkeley, California: Craftways, 1980.

Thomas, Mary. *Mary Thomas's Dictionary of Embroidery Stitches*. New York, N.Y.: Crescent Books, 1989.

Wilson, Erica. *Erica Wilson's Embroidery Book*. New York, N.Y.: Charles Scribner's Sons, 1973.

International Measurements

Approximately Equivalent Measurements

INCHES	CENTIMETERS
1"	2.5cm
2"	5cm
3"	8cm
4"	10cm
5"	13cm
12"	30cm

FEET	METERS
1'	.30 meter
2'	.61 meter
3'	.91 meter

YARDS	METERS
1 yard	.91 meter
2 yards	1.83 meters

COMMON MEASUREMENTS	
1/16"	1.5mm
1/8"	3mm
1/4"	6mm
1/2"	12mm
3/4"	18mm

About the Author

PHOTO: BILL O'CONNOR

udith Montano is a Canadian fiber artist who grew up in the beautiful foothills of the Alberta province. A love of fabrics and embellishments reflects her heritage. Her great-grandmother was a master quilter, and Judith was taught to appreciate needlework at an early age. She attributes the richly embellished and ethnic aspects of her work to growing up on a cattle ranch near an Indian reservation, and later to the eight years she spent overseas in England, Germany, and Japan.

Judith attended the University of California at Chico, graduating with degrees in art and journalism. Upon graduation, she painted with the San Francisco Art Guild. She began quilting in 1976 while living in Houston, Texas, where she was an active member of the Kingswood Quilt Guild.

Judith produced her first prize-winning quilt in 1980, winning Best of Show at the Calgary Exhibition and Stampede in Calgary, Alberta, Canada. It was a special victory for her since her great-grandmother had won the same award in 1934.

"Pekisko Memories," an appliqué quilt depicting her childhood home, which was produced in 1982 in memory of her godfather, won Best of Show at the Texas State Fair, at the Calgary Exhibition and Stampede, and at the Pacific National Exhibition in Vancouver, British Columbia. It won the Mountain Mist award, the Margaret Steel award for design and color, plus many more prizes.

At the same time that she was making quilts, Judith ran a successful antique shop and tea room. For six years people enjoyed her European menu and hospitality in an old, converted church. She closed the shop in 1982 to pursue a career in fiber arts. Her designs soon turned to clothing and crazy quilting. Using rich fabrics, colors, embroideries, beading, and punch needle techniques, her original pieces took on a unique style.

Judith has won many awards for her fiber art. She has done commission work for many national firms such as Concord Fabrics, Fairfield Processing Corporation, Plaid Enterprises, and The Kanagawa Company. Her art garments have appeared in the Fairfield Fashion Shows, traveling throughout the United States, Canada, Europe, and the Far East. She has contributed to the Concord Fabrics' "Cut From The Same Cloth" show plus the Statue of Liberty Fashion Show.

Her work has been featured at the Denver Art Museum, Denver, Colorado; Profiles Gallery, Edmonton, Alberta, Canada; The Dairy Barn, Athens, Ohio; and Mitskoshi Department Show, Tokyo, Japan. She has been a guest artist at the Melbourne Trade Show, Melbourne, Australia; The Tokyo Hobby Show in Tokyo, Japan; and Profiles and Visions, Alberta, Canada.

Judith's designs have been featured in *Quilter's Newsletter Magazine, Quilting U.S.A., Sew Business, Quilting Down Under, Needle Craft For Today, Needle and Thread, Creative Ideas for Living, Lady's Circle Patchwork Quilts, Better Homes and Gardens, Quilts Japan, Craft and Needlework* and *Threads.*

Although her work keeps evolving, crazy quilting always appears in her designs, and she has turned it into a contemporary art form. She is the author of *Crazy Quilt Handbook,* published by C & T Publishers. The book covers history, traditional crazy quilting, embellishments, original designs, and contemporary uses.

Her second book *Crazy Quilt Odyssey, Adventures in Victorian Needlework* takes the reader from traditional Victorian crazy quilting to pictorial punch needle work and silk ribbon embroidery. This third book, *The Art of Silk Ribbon Embroidery,* is a trip down nostalgia lane with full-size patterns, lots of colors, and a complete stitch guide.

Judith has also branched out into the book world as a novelist. Her first fiction novel, *Recollections,* will appear in the spring of 1993.

An accomplished fiber artist, Judith is also a qualified teacher and lecturer. Classes are varied, and she is comfortable in the embroidery, quilting, and fiber arts fields. Teaching has taken her throughout the United States, Canada, Australia, New Zealand, and Japan.

For classes as well as lecture and commission information contact:

Judith Montano, c/o Judith Designs,
P.O. Box 177, Castle Rock, Colorado 80104 U.S.A
Phone & Fax: (303) 660-8072

For book information contact: C & T Publishing,
P.O. Box 1456, Lafayette, California 94549 U.S.A.

Other Fine Quilting Books from C & T Publishing

**For more information write
  for a free catalog from**
C & T Publishing   (1-800-284-1114)
P.O. Box 1456
Lafayette, CA 94549